COMPOSITE NATIONALISM AND ISLAM

Composite Nationalism and Islam

(Muttahida Qaumiyat aur Islam)

MAULANA HUSSAIN AHMAD MADANI

Translated by
Mohammad Anwer Hussain
Hasan Imam

MANOHAR

2023

First published 2005
Reprinted 2006, 2021, 2022, 2023

© Maulana Mahmood Asad Madani, 2005

ISBN 978-81-7304-590-5

Published by
Ajay Kumar Jain *for*
Manohar Publishers & Distributors
4753/23 Ansari Road, Daryaganj
New Delhi 110 002

Printed at
Replika Press Pvt. Ltd.

Contents

Foreword

Although a minority in India, and at times victims of communal frenzy, poor Muslims of partitioned India have grown and matured with the passage of time. Consistent efforts by their adversaries to portray them as the villains of partition failed to have the desired effect on the national canvas. All such efforts paled into insignificance compared to the outstanding contributions made by the Muslims to this great nation. Even though they treated unjustly, discriminated against and prevented from excelling in their natural lingual, cultural and religious environs, the presence of Muslims in all walks of national life is obvious to even an ordinary person.

However, this has not gone down well with a section of the Hindu elite which considers Muslims a different *qaum* (nation) and wants to ensure that they remain socially, politically and economically backward following the migration of a sizeable section to Pakistan. The fact that

their efforts have not produced the desired results
has been a cause of concern for them. Besides, for
them, the irritant is the Muslims' demand for
assertion of their constitutional rights. They,
however, forget the reality that no community
can remain a mute spectator to its plight.
Moreover, the Muslims of free India live here not
just by accident of birth, but also by deliberate
choice. Thus, all talks of projecting them as a
different nation are a thing of the past.

The pertinent question is: Can Indian citizens
co-exist with each other despite their cultural
and religious diversity? Can Hindus, Muslims,
Christians, Sikhs, Buddhists, Zoroastrians and
others live together amicably as one nation? In
view of such incidents as the destruction of the
Babri Masjid and the genocide of Muslims in
Gujarat, this question has assumed paramount
importance.

The book *Muttahida Qaumiyat aur Islam*
translated into English from Urdu by Mohammad
Anwer Hussain and Hasan Imam, is the monograph of a freedom-loving, and a towering religious

and political personality who exhorted Indians to unite, transcending their cultural and religious differences, and fight for freedom from foreign rule under the banner of composite nationalism.

His arguments at the time of British occupation were (and they remain valid in the present-day political scenario as well) that despite being culturally, linguistically and religiously different, people residing in the territorial boundaries of India are but one nation. Any or all efforts to divide them on the basis of caste, colour, creed, culture and religion are a ploy by the ruling power to perpetuate its hegemony and implement its nefarious designs.

The author, Maulana Hussain Ahmad Madani, not only participated in the freedom struggle and served jail sentence, but also spelt out the ethos of Indian nationalism for future generations. It was this ethos that provided vital support to Gandhiji's movement for building 'national unity on the principles of non-discrimination and social justice for all'. As a prominent Indian writer has correctly noted.

the fortitude that the Indian Muslim community has shown in facing the plight of Partition is a great tribute to their patriotism. The Muslims of free India are here not just by accident of birth but by deliberate choice. They rightfully claim the inheritance of their contribution to the making of the Indian nation-state. No small is their contribution to the endeavours for national reconstruction in the wake of the unfortunate Partition.

The patriotism of Indian Muslims is being questioned today. Those who question Muslims' love for this country call themselves 'Hindu' and shout slogans such as *Garv se Kaho Hum Hindu hain*, without understanding that the term 'Hindu' is not the appellation of followers of any religion. It is a geographical definition of a people residing in a territorial region, i.e. India. By virtue of this definition, all people residing within the geographical territory of India, whether they are descendents of Aryans or Dravidians or Mongols or Arabs or Anglo Saxons, are Hindus.

Many writers have noted that the two-nation theory was born more out of political consider-ations than religious concerns. Partition was the result of competition for power between the 'secular' elite of the two communities, rather than justified by the theology of Islam or Hinduism. Any attempt to project the Muslim clergy as separatists would be futile as Muslim religious leaders vehemently opposed the two-nation theory and advocated composite nationalism on religious grounds.

In conclusion, I am inclined to quote a passage from this book that sums up the Muslim mind, the ethos of their faith and their love for this great nation. While participating in the Round Table Conference in London, the veteran freedom fighter Mohammad Ali Jauhar silenced those who had sardonically questioned his integrity as an Indian:

One word as to the Muslim position, with which I shall deal at length on some other occasion. Many people in England ask us why this question of Hindu and Muslim comes into politics, and what it has to do with these things. I reply, It is a wrong conception of religion that you have, if you exclude politics from it. It is not dogma; it is not ritual! Religion, to my mind, means the interpretation of life. I have a culture, a polity, an outlook on life—a complete synthesis which is Islam. Where God commands I am a Muslim first, a Muslim second, and a Muslim last, and nothing but a Muslim. If you ask me to enter into your Empire or into your nation by leaving that synthesis, that polity, that culture, that ethics, I will not do it. My first duty is to my maker, not to H.M. the King. But where India is concerned, where India's freedom is concerned, I am an Indian first, an Indian second, an Indian last, and nothing but an Indian.

I hope and pray that this translated work of Maulana Hussain Ahmad Madani will help in fostering understanding and make people aware of the true concept of nationalism in Islam.

MAULANA MAHMOOD ASAD MADANI
General Secretary
Jamiat Ulama-i-Hind
New Delhi

Preface

Praised be Allah and peace and blessings upon the Prophet

At the behest and insistence of my friends and associates, I issued a statement[1] on the satirical verses composed by Allama Iqbal criticizing my views on the concept of nationalism. Thereafter, I set out for Surat, Haripura, Kawi, Bengal and Assam and remained there for a month. As I was travelling, I had no time to go through the newspapers. I had already expounded the truth of the matter in my statement in Delhi and was hopeful that the misunderstanding and confusion created by some selfish people and the pro-British media would be allayed. When I returned to Deoband[2] and went through old newspapers,

---

[1] In the beginning of Zil-hijja 1356 (twelfth month of Arabic era, AH 1356).

[2] On fifteenth of Muharram AH 1357.

I learnt that my statement had dispelled the misunderstanding among the common people to some extent and had exposed the false propaganda unleashed by the pro-British media. However, my problem increased because of the pressure that I should elaborate my views and stand on composite nationalism.

I read the views of the editor of an Urdu daily *Ehsaan* and Allama Iqbal, as well as letters sent to me by my colleagues soliciting my response. Besides, many friends personally urged me to prepare a strong rebuttal. Since I was preoccupied with my work and was also not keen to write, I was confused about my next step. I did not know whether it would be a good idea to pen my views on the topic or it would be wiser to remain silent. In the meantime, I came across a statement of Allama Iqbal with which he wound up the debate. He wrote:

Hussain Ahmed (Madani) has admitted in some letters to his friends that his statement in Delhi on the subject was in response to the questions of journalists and for the consumption of the press. He had no intention to initiate an academic discussion on the topic. He had simply wanted to convey the fact that in the present time *qaumiyat* of a man is determined by his affiliation to a particular country. And it is a fact that since a long time Europeans and their philosophers have followed are territorial concept of nationalism. I, therefore, wind up this debate here.

Though this statement of Allama Iqbal dispelled all misunderstandings regarding my public statement in Delhi, my restlessness increased because I continued to struggle to give practical shape to the concept of composite nationalism. This is not only my suggestion, I sincerely believe that in the present situation and time it is essential for Indian Muslims. I, therefore, felt it necessary to put forth my views before my countrymen to dispel the misunderstanding and confusion that had been created by my statement on the subject of composite nationalism, which was considered, or at least propagated as, insincere and impermissible.

Since its inception in 1885, the Indian National Congress, has been calling for *Ittehade Qaumi* (national unity) among Indians on the principle of nationalism in order to wage a freedom struggle against the colonial rule. Rival parties and forces opposed to it, on the other hand, made all attempts to denounce the concept of nationalism and brand it as unacceptable and unlawful. Indeed, nothing was more dangerous to the British rule in India than the concept of national unity. This is not a new phenomenon as it has been used ever since 1887 by the British government which has been trying to divide the Indian communities on communal lines and create a chasm between them.

I planned to make public my views on the subject by the end of Muharram. However, extreme preoccupation and unexpected events failed me. I had already started writing and had almost completed explaining the literal meaning of the word *qaumiyat* (nationalism) and was in the process of unravelling the true meaning and connotation of the term, when the news of Allama Iqbal's death reached us. The death of Allama Iqbal saddened me and broke my resolve to write anything more on the topic. Whatever I had written, I thought it proper to keep on the shelf. Though my colleagues urged me to complete the book, I was so heart-broken that I was unwilling to pick up the pen again.

Tor-baithe jab ke hum jam-o-sobu phir hum ko kya
Aasma se badah-o-gulfa'am gar barsa'a kare

When I have already crushed the chalices and vase,
Of no significance, if the sky rained wine and
seductive winds!

When I came to know from the publishers that some people were interested in compiling different writings on the topic of 'composite nationalism' in a booklet, I realized the necessity to place my study and views before the country. I am not so sure that those who have affinity with Great Britain, and whose hearts and minds have been influenced by British thinkers, would accept my views on the subject. Yet, I am hopeful that those who are in search of truth, or those whose hearts and minds are assailed by doubts and confusion, would accept the facts and would certainly benefit from the truth. It was in this context that I began to write this submission. Though in most places the discussion is presented in words and given a definite form, they are related to the comprehensive statement of Allama Iqbal and the writings of the editor of the *Ehsaan*.

There is no denying of the fact that Allama Iqbal was a man of great stature and standing. His achievements were extraordinary. He was a shining star on the horizon of art and philosophy, eloquence and poetry, heart and mind, and other academic and practical fields. Despite all these outstanding qualities, it is not surprising for a man to fall prey to the enchantment of British magicians (read politicians or political thinkers) and misunderstand the real issue. And it is also not surprising that a nursery student is immune to such mistakes.

Ga'ah Bashad Ke Kudake Nada'an
Beghalat Bar Hadaf Zand Teere!

It happens sometimes that an inexperienced child,
Throws arrow and hits the target without any mistake.

Translators' Note

The partition of India into two sovereign states, India and Pakistan, was a watershed in the history of the subcontinent. In the wake of partition, millions of people lost their lives, women were raped, property worth millions was plundered and migration took place from both sides destroying the social fabric of the subcontinent. Partition not only divided the people into two sovereign states, but also divided hearts and irreparably damaged the existing Hindu–Muslim relationship. In the wake, an impression was created by vested interests that Hindus and Muslims were fighting a religious war since centuries (though there has been no such history).

However, a deeper study of the Indian freedom movement proves beyond doubt that the partition was the handiwork of the 'secular' elite of the two communities and not of the religious leaders. Muslim religious scholars not only opposed the two-nation theory, but also supported efforts of the Indian National Congress to thwart the Muslim

League's plan. One of the prominent leaders of the Jamiat Ulama-i-Hind, Maulana Hussain Ahmad Madani, was at the forefront of this movement. He opposed the divisive policy of Mohammad Ali Jinnah and forcefully argued that all communities living in India constitute one nation.

Maulana Hussain Ahmad Madani's statement in Delhi that the basis of modern nations was territorial boundary and not religion became the topic of a heated debate and discussion. Prominent among those who criticized the Maulana's assertions was the great poet and philosopher Mohammad Iqbal. He argued that the concept of territorial nationality was not Islamic and that a nation founded upon kinship, race, language and territory was a curse for humanity.

Arguments and counter-arguments flowed from the two literary giants. Maulana Hussain Ahmad Madani felt the pressing need to write a rejoinder to Iqbal's article because Iqbal's views were likely to do a great deal of harm to the national cause and Hindu–Muslim unity. Thus, Maulana Hussain Ahmad Madani wrote a monograph entitled

Muttahida Qaumiyat aur Islam (*Composite Nationalism and Islam*). This scholarly work mainly deals with two aspects: first, the meaning of the word *qaum* and how it is distinct from the word *millat* and secondly, how the holy Koran and the Hadith tradition view it.

Translating this book was a novel experience for us because the language used in the text is closer to Arabic than Persian that we, in India, are generally used to. Moreover, the circuitous style of conveying a message, with synonyms and repetition of theme with yet another variation of sentence, posed a challenge for us. Though we cannot claim that the translation is free of errors, we are confident that we have successfully rendered the spirit of the Maulana's writing into the English language.

This translation could have never been realized without the generous help we have received from many sides. First of all we would like to thank Hazrat Maulana Asad Madani, President of Jamiat Ulama-i-Hind, for his encouragement. Without his sincere *dua* this work could not have been completed.

Our special thanks are due to Maulana Mahmood Asad Madani, General Secretary of Jamiat Ulama-i-Hind, for his generous encouragement and assistance in getting the work published. Without his moral support this book could not have seen the light of the day.

The translators wish to express their deep sense of gratitude to Professor Barbara D. Metcalf for writing the Introduction and for giving valuable suggestions.

We are especially grateful to Maulana Badruddin Ajmal Al-Qasmi, Chairman of Markazul Ma'arif (Mumbai), for his generous encouragement with financial and manpower support, and for considering us competent and assigning to us the task of translating the book.

We are thankful to Allah Subhanahu Wa Ta'la for it is He who gets things done by His servants. For any shortcomings in this translation, we accept all responsibility.

MOHAMMAD ANWER HUSSAIN
HASAN IMAM

Introduction

BARBARA D. METCALF

Maulana Hussain Ahmad Madani (1879–1957) may well have made the most influential and significant intervention in religious thought of any Islamic scholar of twentieth century India. Certainly there were other luminous figures among the learned. Maulana Ashraf 'Ali Thanawi (1864–1943) was a prolific writer and eminent spiritual guide who substantially furthered the work of traditionalist reform. Maulana Abu'l Kalam Azad (1888–1958) was a towering intellectual and statesman. Similarly, Maulana Abu'l Hasan 'Ali Nadwi (1914–99), a generation later, not only played a significant public role within India, but was also institutionally and intellectually engaged with the Muslim world beyond India. The originality of Abul A'la Maududi (1903–79), known for his 'Islamist' religious thought forged in the pre-independence decades, is undisputed, but his influence is significant largely outside India. Maulana Madani is not as well known as these others to a large part of the English-speaking world, and his key writings, compared to those they produced, were, relatively few. The importance of his writings lies in the fact that they laid out in uncompromising terms, the Islamic sanction for Muslims to work and live with non-Muslims in a shared polity, and, specifically, to embrace the secular democracy of a state like India. For that reason, the translation at hand of one of his most important works is particularly valuable.

WORLD WAR I AND ITS AFTERMATH

The work translated in this volume, *Muttahida Qaumiyat aur Islam* (*Composite Nationalism and Islam*) was written in 1938. It laid out in systematic form positions that Maulana Madani had taken in speeches and letters from the early 1920s. At that point, a new public life had begun to appear in India thanks to two significant transformations: First, the impact of the First World War. India suffered in the War both from internal economic disruptions and loss of life from heavy military deployments in Europe. Politically conscious Indians, of whom Madani was one, were, moreover, horrified at the devastation that Europe had wrought. Second, during the War, Indians had been promised progress toward the self-determination that was a central diplomatic theme of the times. Disappointing in scope though it was, a second Councils Act in 1919 (following on one issued in 1909) increased Indian participation in elections and councils and stimulated a new level of political organizing. At the same time, humiliating and repressive emergency legislation was passed by the colonial power that brought home just how limited political advance had been.

For Madani, the War years had been particularly significant. Till that point, his life had been that of a typical Islamic scholar associated with the traditionalist reform of the Darul Ulum, Deoband (founded in 1867). He had Sufi initiation by one of the school's great founding spiritual guides, and he was particularly devoted to one of the second generation of great teachers at the school, Maulana Mahmood Hasan (1851–1920). A significant dimension of his life in contrast to that of most other Deobandis, however, was that his father had emigrated to Madina, so that, although punctuated by travel back to India, Madani from an early age was primarily based in the Hejaz. When Mahmood Hasan came to Madina in 1915, Madani became involved with his teacher's association to people engaged in what came to be known as 'The Silk Letter Conspiracy'. These activists were among those who saw the War years as an opportunity to challenge colonial rule militarily. (Muslims were not alone in this. There were similar efforts in Bengal as well as one that linked Punjab and San Francisco.) This stance, it is worth noting, was a dramatic break with the loyalism of the day, as characteristic of those at Deoband as it was, for example, of the Indian National Congress (which had been founded in 1885). This particular 'conspiracy' seems to have imagined links with Ottomans and Afghans who would join with freedom-lovers in India to oust the colonial rulers.

Madani, Mahmood Hasan, and several others were arrested and interned in Malta for almost four years.

Like colonial prisons everywhere, Malta was a school for radicalism and an occasion for forming new types of social ties. As Madani described life on Malta from 1916 to 1920 in his *Prisoner of Malta (Asir-i Malta)* (1923), he interacted with Germans, Austrians, Turks and other Indians, including one Bengali Brahmin accused of manufacturing bombs, all arrested for being opponents of the British, whether as military enemies or colonial rulers. Madani, like so many others in such circumstances, saw internment as an occasion to study and talk to other prisoners, free of colonial surveillance. This prison experience marked a watershed in his life. Instead of growing old in Madina, as he might have, Madani subsequently moved permanently to India. There he became Principal of the school at Deoband; he helped organize Muslims to firmly support the Congress party; and he was periodically imprisoned.

The key issue that led Mahmood Hasan and

Madani, along with others of the 'ulama, into political life was a campaign in 1919–20 in support of the Turkish khilafat. The post-War dismemberment of the Ottoman Empire was seen by Indians as a symbol of British colonial perfidy, a betrayal of an explicit Wartime commitment to Muslim subjects in particular that the Empire would not be dismembered. In that sense, the movement to preserve the caliphate was less about the Ottomans than about India, with the fate of the Ottomans conflated with India's own. This was, for example, a reason that non-Muslims like Gandhi found the movement plausible. It is fair to say, however, that Khilafat leaders failed to see the strength of Arab and Turkish nationalism, forces with which in principle they should have been sympathetic. The Turks themselves in 1924 abolished the caliphate. Nonetheless, the movement gave Westernized Muslim leaders a kind of 'Islamic' rather than only a 'Muslim community', or interest-based, identity. It also drew popular Muslim participation into political movements for the first time. It marked a new role for the traditionally educated 'ulama, including Maulana Madani. And it established a model for Muslim participation in public life.

The Khilafat movement set the path for what would endure as a pattern for Muslim participation in the nationalist movement. It entailed whole heartedly embracing Gandhi's leadership, with an acceptance of the new strategy of non-cooperation with British rule and the goal of complete freedom before even the Indian National Congress did so. Political action represented parallel participation of two organizations, not single action comprising individuals. In that sense, the first 'mass contact' movement brought Muslims into political life as Muslims. Muslims thus had shared goals with the larger nationalist movement, but entered them as a separate unit, as Muslims with their own organization.

It is noteworthy that Gandhi encouraged Hindus to support the Khilafat movement *not* on the issue of British perfidy in relation to the Ottomans, a 'non-religious' issue, but rather on the need for Muslims and Hindus to support each other's distinctive concerns: 'to-day, seeing that the Mohammedans are deeply touched on the question of the Khilafat and their cause is just, nothing can be so powerful for winning Mohammedan friendship for the Hindu as to give his whole-hearted support to the claim' (quoted in Andrews, 1949, p. 59). The Khilafat movement thus reinforced the understanding of society as consisting of a 'partnership' of bounded units.

Madani's commitment to working with non-Muslims in independent India, articulated in the 1938 work published here, had by then stood many tests. When the new Association of Indian Ulama, the Jamiat Ulama-i-Hind (a forum founded in 1919 to speak for Muslims and support the movement for independence) bravely embraced Gandhi's first Non-Cooperation movement in 1921, Madani and several others of the leadership faced two years of imprisonment for 'conspiracy'. Nonetheless, harmony between Hindus and Muslims was short-lived. By February 1922 following the unexpected violence at Chauri Chaura the first Non-Cooperation movement collapsed. The subsequent decade witnessed brutal violence between Hindus and Muslims and energetic proselytizing campaigns by both.

More subtly, as recent scholarship has unveiled in often surprising ways, in the decades preceding independence even those committed to Muslim participation in political life espoused ideas about Muslims and Indian civilization that are usually associated with the Hindu ethnonationalism of the Mahasabha, the RSS (founded in 1925), and their subsequent heirs. Key Congress socialists, usually thought of as 'the left', in fact often had close connections with the Arya Samaj and Hindu cultural revivalism, espousing an organic view of Hinduism like that of extreme Hindu nationalists of the time (Gould, 2002).

Virtually all public figures accepted the narrative of Indian history that posited Muslims as foreign invaders and marauders. Vernacular novels in Bengali and Marathi, for example, imagined a past of heroic Hindu peoples defying Muslim tyrants.

Indeed, the narrative was internalized by Muslim writers as well (Chatterjee, 1993, pp. 75–115). Professional historians deny the historical validity of such narratives. No Muslim monarch had a programme of conversion; all polities were based on networks of loyalty in which religion was irrelevant; all rulers, Hindu and Muslim, selectively looted or destroyed temples and other religious sites of political opponents and then patronized them during settled conditions (Eaton, 2001). Sanskrit studies and religious styles like *bhakti* flourished under Muslim rule. Yet the narrative of Muslim aggression and destruction is so 'natural', as anthropologist Peter van der Veer has written, that it is virtually unassailable (van der Veer, 2002).

A corollary view in the nationalist imagination was that the presence of Muslims, and secondarily Christians, was the product of violent coercion, whether physical or economic. In this view 'being a Hindu' is taken as the 'natural identity'. In fact, a historian could argue, the presence of today's Hindu population is as much linked to the activities of saints, traders and soldiers among nomads and tribals (who were not 'Hindu' to begin with) as is the presence of Islam (Eaton, 1993; van der Veer, 2002). But it was the contrary view that fuelled the *Shuddhi* movement of putative 'reconversion' that dominated the 1920s. Nowhere did the notions of Hinduism and nationalism come together more powerfully than in the writings of the Hindu militant and ideologue, Vinayak Damodar Savarkar (1883–1966) who insisted that India was a Hindu land, sacred only to Hindus and not to so-called 'foreign' Muslims and Christians. Muslims had no ties with India, he insisted: their holy places were all in Arabia just as Christian holy places were all in Palestine (Savarkar, 1923, pp. 293–5).

Maulana Madani, one might note, countered this narrative of Indian history in two ways. One was to place the spread of Hinduism after the establishment of Muslim dynasties and not before, emphasizing the minor place of Brahmanical institutions in contrast to Buddhist influence at least in the regions of the north and north-west (Madani, 1950–1, I, pp. 141–9). A second was to delineate the ways in which India was in fact a sacred land to Muslims, not least because of the descent of Adam to Ceyon from paradise, the early

presence of prophetic companions in the subcontinent, and the centuries of burials of saints
and holy men whose charismatic presence conti-
nues till today (Madani, 1941, pp. 1–6). These
arguments found little 'traction' at their time or
after, given, as noted earlier, how unassailable the
colonial-period narrative of Muslims as destructive
foreigners had become.

Madani spent the years after his release from
prison firm in his commitment to national unity
and active in influencing Jamiat policy. The commitment to working closely with the Indian
National Congress was strengthened when the
Congress declared complete independence as its
goal in 1930, and he supported the second Non-
Cooperation movement launched in the same year.

THE CONTEXT OF THE DEBATE
OVER *QAUM* AND *MILLAT*

Yet another change in the context for political
activities came in the mid-1930s with the enlarged
electorates and substantial extension of provincial

autonomy granted by the 1935 Government of India Act. Congress won stunning victories, establishing ministries in seven provinces, including the United Provinces. There, however, the Muslim League had won all 29 of the reserved seats for Muslims and the Congress had won none. The decision not to include the League in a coalition, and a range of other perceived slights and policies, definitively alienated many of the Muslim leadership, including Maududi, from Congress support.

Madani's case was different. He had in fact supported Mohammad Ali Jinnah's Muslim League in the 1937 elections, a reflection of their shared devotion to Indian nationalism and to securing the interests of Muslims at a time when the vision of independence was still very fluid and the Congress and the League might still have found ways to cooperate. Jinnah had apparently made a commitment to shift the direction from the party away from its core support of aristocratic and—in Madani's view—pro-British members in favour of anti-British nationalists, including 'ulama like himself. But Madani soon perceived Jinnah's continued support of princes and big landlords, coupled with his failure to consult with the 'ulama, as a betrayal (Madani, 1950–1, I, p. 384). Instead of the Muslim League and the Indian National Congress coming closer, they increasingly diverged. Not only did the claim of the League to be the only representative of Muslims intensify, but also increasingly articulated demands for Muslim geographic autonomy. In contrast, Madani ever more clearly formulated his arguments for Muslim and non-Muslim politicians to work together under the aegis of the Indian National Congress. Madani was absolutely clear that his vision of a religiously plural society not only strategically best served Muslim interests, but that it also had clear Koranic sanction.

As recounted in the text translated here, the occasion for writing his definitive statement of this position, might have seemed a tempest in a tea-pot, based on a misunderstanding that was met with clever, vitriolic verses by the failing, but still acerbic, poet Mohammad Iqbal. In fact, the debate went far beyond the immediate cause, and each of the protagonists used this contretemps to make a definitive statement of his respective position. The 'misunderstanding' made clear that fundamental cleavages had emerged in thinking about the future of Muslim political life in the subcontinent.

In December 1937, at a political meeting in Delhi, Maulana Madani made a straightforward statement, 'In the current age, nations (*qaumeen*) are based on homelands (*autaan*, pl. of *watn*), not religion (*mazhab*).' What made this point obvious to him was that people abroad made no distinction of whether a person was 'Muslim, Hindu, Sikh or Parsi'—all were viewed as 'Hindustani'. He reiterated as he often had before, all Indians were viewed with contempt because of being in bondage to colonial rule. The following day Urdu newspapers *al-Aman* and *Ehsaan* (soon followed by others) had reported that Maulana Madani had said that not 'nation', but *millat* (a term commonly in fact linked to religious community) depended on territory. Madani had not said that, but the report provided Iqbal an opportunity to insist that

Muslims needed a political unit or units of their own, an opinion he shared with people like Maududi and Jinnah (for all their differences).

Iqbal, although in the throes of what would be his final illness, was quick to respond. His reply consisted of three Persian verses:

> The non-Arab world *still* does not know the secrets of the faith
> Thus from Deoband Hussain Ahmad proves somewhat strange singing out high on the pulpit
> *That* millat *is based on land* [watan].

> *What* does he know of the stance of the Arab Messenger, on whom be peace?
> Bring yourself close to Mustafa, for his alone is faith complete

> If you cannot approach him
> *You're just an Abu Lahab!*

Now this was quite a verse. It was of course a scandalous slander. It suggested quite simply that Maulana Madani, a resident of the non-Arab world or *Ajam*, did not know Arabic—and this about someone who had had the highest training in the classical Arabic disciplines, was Principal of the most respected seminary in India, and a scholar participate in Arabic who had long been resident in the Prophet's own Arab city of Madina. Second, it mocked his political role, placing him on a 'pulpit'—and 'singing' [*surod*] no less—when in fact he had been addressing a public meeting. Perhaps worst of all, it implied that Maulana Madani, whether spiritually or in terms of behaviour, was far from the Prophet, identified first as the 'Arab Messenger', to stress language, and then as 'Mustafa', 'the Chosen', to underline Mohammad's uniqueness. All this, by implication, implied that unless he changed, Maulana Madani was a veritable 'Abu Lahab', the 'Father of the Flame', the nickname for the Prophet's uncle who had rejected him early in his prophecy and was consigned in the Koran 'to roast at a flaming fire' (*Sura* CXI). For the most part Iqbal had little respect for the traditionalist 'ulama, let alone contemporary Sufi pirs, who lacked he believed his own modernist, dynamic vision of movement and change. That, too, made him perhaps ready to mount an attack like this.

Maulana Madani's subsequent letter underlined that religion and *millat* were certainly not dependent on homeland or territory, and that he had spoken not of *millat* but of *qaum* (Madani, 1950–1, III, pp. 123–42.) Iqbal's reply on 9 March 1938, published in *Ehsaan*, made clear, however, that his challenge to Maulana Madani was not a matter of vocabulary but a fundamental difference about the basis of political community in general and the strategies before the Muslims of India in particular.

WHAT IQBAL SAID AND WHY HE SAID IT

Iqbal dismissed the distinction between *millat* and *qaum* as a philological quibble, irrelevant to his fundamental concern, namely, his denunciation of the modern, territorially based nationalism modelled by Europe that he believed was destructive of ideal human relationships as symbolized by Islam (Iqbal, 1973, pp. 234–5). In poetry and prose, he had for decades, in company with a minor strand of other Indian intellectuals as well as with European and non-European critics across the globe, denounced the 'black' side of modernity: competitive nationalism and its resultant militarism, imperialism and consumerism. As he wrote in his response to Maulana Madani, 'I have been repudiating the concept of Nationalism since the time when it was not well-known in India and the Muslim world' (Iqbal, 1973, p. 230). Just as Madani saw the hand of imperialism in tearing apart plural societies on religious grounds (as Muslims and Christians) in the Ottoman Empire, Iqbal emphasized the same intervention as sowing the seeds of national boundaries between Arabs and Turks who should have realized their common bonds as Muslims.

Iqbal had, he said, no quarrel with simple patriotism: '...the Maulana's statement that nations are formed by lands, is not open to objections' (Iqbal, 1938, p. 231). It was when that simple love of native land became a 'political concept' or 'social order' that he objected in favour of an order based on Islam. Nationalism, Iqbal believed, inevitably led to indifference towards religion, as had happened in Europe. The Maulana might claim that *millat* had a higher place than religious community, as he had done in his response, but his approach, according to Iqbal, would lead to religion as 'a merely private affair, (Iqbal, 1938, p. 235). Iqbal insisted that his was the correct reading of the Koran, whose only call was to the *millat* or *ummat* of Islam. Iqbal accepted the point made by Madani that a *qaum* could include believers and non-believers, but only to insist on the higher prophetic goal of creating the *umma* of believers that transcended the destructive divisions of nation and race. The Prophet rejected those of his own lineage—like Abu Lahab—who denied Islam. The Prophet in short was not an Arab patriot but a leader of co-religionists (Iqbal, 1938, pp. 242–3).

In concluding his statement, far from glossing over the differences between them, Iqbal went beyond the insult of his original verse. He went so far as to identifiy the ideas of 'Maulana Hussain Ahmad and others who think like him' as being as egregiously deviant as those of the modern sect, the Ahmadiyya (or as he called them 'Qadiani').

The Ahmadis were alleged to deny the fundamental Islamic tenet of the finality of Prophet Mohammad. The idea of nationalism might be political, Iqbal wrote, and the idea of prophethood theological, but both, he argued '[took] up a position in addition to what the divine law [had] prescribed and defined for them for all time to come'. For Madani, an active voice in virulent opposition to the Ahmadis, this was a low blow indeed. Between the poet and the Maulana there was indeed a gulf.

Iqbal and Madani did not differ over the basis of nationalism, the one insisting on religion, the other on territory, as it might seem. The real point was that Iqbal, unrealistically, struggled to imagine a world in the twentieth century *with no nationalism at all*. He thought that Muslim political autonomy would foster in one place a less divided and less exploitative society on the basis of an Islamic moral system that would in fact serve all people, Muslim or non-Muslim.

Nor did they share a view of Islam. 'Islam' then as now meant various things to different people.

Modernist to the core, for Iqbal, Islam was a great philosophical system, nothing less than the very source of modernity. This was an issue of no interest whatsoever to Madani. Iqbal imagined a genealogy of rationalism that produced modern science, and in that genealogy Muslims had played a substantial role, not merely as transmitters of the classical heritage to Europe but as active participants and shapers of that heritage. Indeed in one of the striking passages of the celebrated series of lectures he delivered in 1928, he turned to the Prophet of Islam who, he maintained, 'in so far as the spirit of his revelation is concerned ... belongs to the modern world.... The birth of Islam ... is the birth of inductive intellect' (Iqbal, 1928, p. 126). In his vision, moreover, the rational, ethical system of Islam was to be understood precisely by individuals like himself, without 'priesthood and hereditary kingship', given 'the constant appeal to reason and experience in the Koran, and the emphasis that it [laid] on Nature and History as sources of human knowledge' (Iqbal, 1928, p. 126). In a place rid of colonialism as well as of nationalist and other divisions, the spirit of Islam would allow a society of creative individuals to flourish again.

It is worth underlining what his stance in relation to Islam was not. It was not the 'Islamist' vision emerging in these decades, associated above all with Maududi, that made Islam an alternate to totalizing systems like fascism and communism. Nor was it concerned with disseminating fidelity to the ritual and social practices of Islamic law, the concern of reformist 'ulama like Madani. His lack of concern for 'Islamic law' or an 'Islamic system', was evident in his 1930 presidential address to the Muslim League:

Nor should the Hindus fear that the creation of autonomous Muslim states will mean the introduction of a kind of religious rule in such states.... It is a state conceived as a contractual organism long before Rousseau ever thought of such a thing....The character of a Muslim state can be judged from what the *Times of India* pointed out some time ago in a leader on the Indian Banking Enquiry Committee. 'In ancient India', the paper points out, 'the state framed laws regulating the rates of interest, but in Muslim times, although

Islam clearly forbids the realization of interest on money loaned, Indian Muslim states imposed no restriction on such notes.' (Iqbal, 1930, pp. 14–15)

This speech is better known for being the first influential call for autonomy, in this case within India, of areas of Muslim concentration like Punjab and the north-west where he hoped his Islamic vision could flourish. That the seed he watered with these remarks would grow into the virulently nationalist state of Pakistan is surely one of the great ironies of twentieth century history.

MAULANA MADANI'S REPLY

At least three themes resonate in both Maulana Madani's letter and his extended answer to Iqbal, translated here. First, Maulana Madani implicitly asserted his own authority as someone with the classical training of the 'ulama the foundation of whose learning was correct understanding of the Arabic language. Iqbal had claimed with a poetic verse to have better understanding of the Koran: the qalandar knows only two words of Arabic—*la ilaha*—in contrast to the jurist with his vast vocabulary. He thus married an old Sufi trope to the modernist styles of interpetation of sacred texts without concern for the historic tradition of interpretation. Maulana Madani did, indeed, proceed exactly as a traditional scholar would. He entitled the first substantive subheading of the work below: 'The Key to Koranic Vocabulary and the Words of Hadith will Come Only from the Arabic Tongue' (Madani, n.d., p. 7). Approximately the first half of this treatise meticulously examined texts, provided both in Arabic and Urdu translation, scrutinized in the light of Arabic usage as known from grammars and dictionaries of the Prophet's own time. In the light of this scholarly approach, he denied what he saw as Iqbal's equation of *qaum* and *millat*. He established that in the Prophet's usage a *qaum* could consist of believers and unbelievers both of whom who act together for a common purpose—and that would be the model for the *qaum* of India.

A second critical theme that Maulana Madani set out in the text, lest Iqbal be allowed to impute otherwise, was his full embrace of the classic belief that Islam was the final revelation intended for all humankind. This, in his own subheading, he termed the 'intrinsic' or 'inner' (*m'anavi*) import of issues related to *qaumiyat* precisely this universal audience (Madani, n.d., p. 22). All people may not, to be sure, accept this message (Madani, n.d., p. 23). As for the bonds among those who follow Islam, they are, he argues, the basis for the greatest unity among humans that can exist, the unity of the *millat*, *milli wahdat*. Maulana Madani imagines independent India as a place where Islamic learning and cultural traditions, like his, will be protected and where the message of Islam, whether accepted or not, will be available to all.

Third, Maulana Madani reiterated his stance on the nature of colonial rule since it was clear to him that Iqbal's position served only imperial interests. Central to his argument, as noted earlier, was his emphasis on the machinations of the colonial rulers in fostering divisions of race (*nasl*) and homeland (*watan*) in the Ottoman Empire as what he feared would happen again with the

division of India. To do this, the British praised
nationalism raised against the Ottomans but
subsequently deplored it when it united Hindus
and Muslims in India under the pretext of securing
the safety of Muslims. Madani refused this argument. Muslims and non-Muslims were already
working to secure common goals in politics and
other arenas of life. That pattern had, moreover,
an analogue in an episode in the life of Prophet
Mohammad, the Treaty of Hudaibiyah, when he
allied with various non-Muslims, including Jews.
In such a compact, Madani argued, a Muslim
would side with non-Muslims even against a
common Muslim foe.

In turning to Madani's goal of an independent
India, central to his thinking was his emphasis
on communities relatively encapsulated in their
individual languages, cultures, education and
moral/legal systems. It is in this sense that Madani's
conviction about the importance of language,
noted earlier, has importance. The commitments
he details from the Indian National Congress,
reiterated below, served, he believed to secure

these rights. Historian Peter Hardy has spoken of this vision as a kind of 'judicial' or we could even say cultural, 'apartheid' (Hardy, 1971). He imagined Muslims as a 'community', guided by religious leadership, following distinctive educational, cultural, and legal paths from other religiously defined communities. What was left for common efforts, Madani argued, were effectively those now delegated to a range of public forums and assemblies. The risk to Islam he feared was not from interacting with Hindus but from the British given their policies and their style of English education. It was with a hard-headed appraisal of the destructiveness of British rule and the need to overthrow it that Madani ended his pamphlet.

Maulana Madani was a hard-headed pragmatist. He recognized that nationalism, democracy, and the importance of public opinion were the political currency of the day. He welcomed that form of government as a context in which an 'ulama like himself could guide Muslims in all those practices of faith and work that made up the texture of an observant religious life. His was not the 'spirit' of philosophical, ethical Islam of Iqbal, but the concrete Islam of individual ritual and behavioural guidance. He shared the pattern of 'traditionalist' Islamic leaders elsewhere as well who welcome a secular state that gives them scope to further that guidance. Madani could not imagine severing his ties with the plural society he lived in and the land where his ancestors were buried. He could not imagine a state led by irreligious people like Jinnah or one led by ideologues like Maududi, who seemed oblivious of the astonishing diversity of Muslim sectarian orientations and of a political culture predicated on persuasion, not force.

If Iqbal had no way to predict the shape of Pakistan, Madani had no way to predict that independent India would come into being with two-thirds of the Muslim population, and all five majority provinces gone. Part of his confidence in the future of Muslims in India, as he clearly indicates here, had been based on their substantial numbers. In the horrific aftermath of partition, however, Madani did not waiver from his belief in the future of Muslims in India, as he indicated in his presidential address to the Jamiat in 1948 he called on his co-religionists to devote themselves to the service of their country and engage in the 'great jihad', *jihad-i akbar* (the greater *jihad*) of moral struggle and honing of one's character.

If Madani has a lasting legacy to Muslims in India today, one might suggest that it is precisely his pragmatism, coupled with *jihad-i akbar*, that should be embraced. Such pragmatism would require continuous reflection on whether the strategies adopted more than half a century ago in relation to Muslim community life best serve Muslims in India today, the country of their birth and loyalty, in these rapidly changing times.

REFERENCES

Andrews, Charles Freer. 1949 [1929]. *Mahatma Gandhi's Ideas: Including Selections from His Writings.* London: George Allen and Unwin.

Chatterjee, Partha. 1993. *The Nation and Its Fragments: Colonial and Postcolonial Histories.* Princeton: Princeton University Press.

Eaton, Richard M. 1993. *The Rise of Islam and the Bengal*

Frontier, 1204-1760. Berkeley: University of California Press.

———2001. 'Temple Desecration and Indo-Muslim States', _Frontline_ (India), 17, 26 (23 Dec. 2000–5 Jan. 2001), pp. 70–7.

Hardy, Peter. 1971. _Partners in Freedom and True Muslims: Thought of Some Muslim Scholars in British India, 1912-47._ Lund: Scandinavian Institute of Asian Studies.

Iqbal, Mohammad. 1930. 'Presidential address delivered at the annual session of the All-India Muslim League at Allahabad, 29 December 1930', in Iqbal, 1948, pp. 3–36.

———1938. 'Statement on Islam and Nationalism in Reply to a Statement of Maulana Hussain Ahmad', _Ehsaan_, 9 March 1938; in Iqbal, 1948, pp. 229–46.

———1973. Speeches and Statements of Iqbal. Compiled by Sh. Ghulam Ali and Sons, Lahore.

———ed. 1978 [1928]. _The Reconstruction of Religious Thought in Islam._ Lahore: Sh. Mohammad Ashraf.

Madani, Hussain Ahmad. 1923. _Asir-i Malta_, Deoband Company, n.d.

———n.d. [1938]. _Muttahida Qaumiyat aur Islam (Composite Nationalism and Islam)._ New Delhi: Jamiat Ulama-i-Hind.

————1953. *Naqsh-i Hayat* (Impression of a Life), 2 vols. With an Introduction by Maulana Hifz ur-Rahman. Deoband: Maktaba diniyya.

————1950/51. *Maktubat-i Shaikhu'l-Islam* (Letters of Shaikhu'l Islam), 4 vols. Ed. and Introduction by Maulana Najmu'd-din Islahi with a Foreword by Maulana Qari Mohammad Tayyib Qasimi et al. Deoband: Maktaba diniyya.

————1988. *Intikhab Khutbat Jami'at Ulama-i Hind (Selection of Sermons/Addresses to the Jamiat Ulama-i-Hind)*. Ed. Shuja'at 'Ali Sandelvi. Lucknow: Uttar Pradesh Urdu Akadmi.

————1941. *Hamara Hindustan aur uske Fazail* (India: Our Land and Its Virtues). Trans. Mohammad Anwer Hussain. New Delhi: Jamiat Ulama-i-Hind.

Savarkar, Vinayak Damodar. 1923. *Hindutva: In Sources of Indian Tradition*, vol. 2, 2nd edn. Ed. Stephen Hay. New York: Columbia University Press, 1988, pp. 289–95.

van der Veer, Peter. 2002. 'Traditions of Violence in South Asia'. Paper presented at the international conference on 'Living Together Separately: Cultural India in History and Politics', 19–21 December 2002, Jamia Millia Islamia, New Delhi.

The Reality of My Delhi Speech and Spreading of the News of Composite Nationalism

As Allama Iqbal learnt from my replies to some of my friends' letters, I had no intention of advising any one on Nationalism and I had used no such words in the statement I had issued in Delhi. I was simply talking about the great loss and sufferings that the British government has inflicted upon all Indians, especially Muslims. I also mentioned the fact that in our times the country makes a nation. And that all Indians, whether they be Hindu, Muslim, Sikh or Zoroastrian, are looked down upon everywhere abroad. Since they all belong to this country, they are regarded as one *qaum*. Their prestige and honour is no better than that of slaves: they are treated shabbily and their legitimate demands are ignored. Indians are not only discriminated against abroad regarding their citizenship rights, but are also discriminated against vis-à-vis their human rights. All their protests fall on deaf ears. This is, in my view, an effect of slavery.

How the cronies of the British government would have digested such remarks! They blew them out of proportion and made a mountain out of a molehill. However, there may be some hidden virtues behind this euphoria. If seen from this perspective, the discussion is over. Seen from another angle, I deem it necessary to say something because, according to Allama Iqbal, any counsel of composite nationalism to Indian Muslims is unethical and un-Islamic—which in my view is not correct. During the course of my explanation, I have discussed some other aspects related to the issue which I had pointed out briefly in my previous statement, and which I have been asked by many to explain again.

Only an Arabic Language Dictionary can Interpret the Koranic Words and the Hadith

The Almighty Allah did not send Prophets to invent a new language. They substituted the prevalent wrong traditions with a right one among those tribes and nations for whom they were directed and sent. They came on earth and addressed their nations in their native languages, which the people used everyday.

FIRST ARGUMENT

Allah says in the holy Koran:

> 'And We never sent a messenger save with the language of his folk....' (14. 4)

THE SECOND ARGUMENT

Says the Almighty in the holy Koran:

> 'O mankind! The messenger hath come unto you with the truth from your Lord. Therefore believe; (it is) better for you.' (4. 170)

Thus, it would be essential to search for all the Commandments of Allah and the views of the Prophets in their language itself. One would have to rely on their understanding of the language.

To give a new meaning to a word that is not part of the coverage of that nation would be a grave mistake. For this reason I have quoted certain Arabic dictionaries briefly to explain the meaning of the words *qaum* and *millat,* and have advised (readers) to refer to the verses of the holy Koran and the sayings of the Prophet. Since the matter did not end there, I have furnished more details.

It is written in the *Mukhtarus Seha*[1] (Chapter *Lam, Mim and Noon*) that the word *millat* means sharia (religion). Again it is said (Chapter *Mim,* Section *Qaf*):

The word *millat* means sharia and as per Chapter *Mim,* Section *Qaf*: the word *qaum* denotes men, barring women, and the word *qaum* does not have any singular form. Zohair says that I do not know whether the tribe of *hisn* is *qaum* (nation) or women.

The Glorious Koran goes on to says,

'Let not a folk deride a folk who may be better than they are. Nor let women deride women who may be better than they (are).' (49. 11)

---

[1] An Arabic grammar book.

Thus, at some places in the holy Koran, women-folk have been automatically subsumed in the concept of *qaum* (nation) because both men as well as women comprise the *qaum* of all the Prophets.

The Chapter *Lam*, Section *Mim* of *Qamus* (*Sharh-e-Qamus* and *Tajul Oroos of Zubaidi*)[2] says,

The word *millat* means sharia or *deen*. For example, Religion of Islam, Religion of Jews and Religion of Christians, etc. Some other experts are of the opinion that the word *millat* applies to the major portion of a religion and things brought out by a Prophet, and the argument of *Raghib* points out that all three are the synonyms of *millat*.

According to the *Raghib*, *millat* means that particular thing which the Almighty Allah has revealed to the people through the Prophets so that they can come closer to Him. And the difference between the words *millat* and *deen* is that the word *millat* is attributed to the Prophet and his people for whom he has been sent. The word

---

[2] An Arabic dictionary.

millat cannot be attributed to the Almighty Allah or to any (pious) individual.

Abu Ishaque[3] says that the literal meaning of the word *millat* is 'the saying and doing' of a Prophet, and that the word *millat* is derived from there. This also refers to a place where bread is eaten.

According to As'as, calling *millat* a path that has been followed before is, in a metaphoric sense, as it is said, that the *Millat-e-Ibrahim* (the nation of Abraham) is among the best nations.

As per the *Qamus* (Chapter *Mim*, Section *Qaf*) the word *qaum* embraces both men and women, or only men where women are automatically included.

In the *Tajul Uroos*[4] the word *qaum* includes both men and women because the *qaum* of an individual (leader) are his followers. Or, the word *qaum* means a group of men only, exclusive of women. The word *qaum* has no singular use.

---

[3] A great linguist of the Arabic language.
[4] A commentary of *Qamus*.

According to *jauhari*[5] it is as per the second set of meaning that the glorious Koran asks a *qaum* not to laugh at another *qaum*.[6] Again, it is said that no group of women should scoff at other women. If women were included in *qaum*, there was no need of saying: '*Wala Nisaun Min Nisa*'.

Zaheer[7] mentions in one of his Arabic verses, 'I do not know but soon I may come to know whether the tribe of Hisn are *qaum* (men) or women.'

A Hadith (saying) of Prophet Mohammad elucidates that if an *imam* (a leader of prayer) commits a mistake while leading a congregation, the *qaum* (meaning 'men') will say '*Subhanallah*' (glory be to Allah) and the women will beat their palms as an indication of the mistake.

According to *Ibn-e-Asir*[8] says that the word

---

[5] A famous linguist.

[6] 'O ye who believe! Let not some men (*qaum*) among you laugh at others. It may be that the latter are better than the former. Nor let some women laugh at others. It may be that the latter are better than the former' (49. 11).

[7] A distinguished poet of classical Arabic literature.

[8] An expert of Arabic language.

qaum is derived from the word *qama* which is frequently used to refer to men, excluding women. The explanation is that the word 'man' are syn-onymous with *qaum* because they (men) are responsible for those affairs of women that the latter are incapable of handling.

Abul Abbas has been quoted as saying that the three words *qaum* (nation), *nafar* (group) and *rahat* (band) connote a plural meaning and no singular meaning can be derived from them. And that these words are used either exclusively for men, or womenfolk are automatically included in them because the *qaum* of every Prophet comprises both men and women.

The word *qaum* is used for both masculine and feminine gender because those plural nouns from which singular cannot be derived, if used only in the sense of human beings, are used for both masculine as well as feminine genders. For example, with regard to the words *rahat*, *nafar* and *qaum*, the Almighty Allah says, '*Wa Kaziba Behi Qaumak.*' Here, the word *qaum* is used as masculine. Every-where, Allah says, '*Kazzabat Qauma Nuh Al-*

Mursaleen.' Here, the word *qaum* is used as feminine.

The *Majma-ul-Bahar* mentions that the word *millat* means the sharia that has been given to a nation by the Almighty Allah through the Prophet. The word *millat* applies to the sharia in toto. It does not apply to a section. For example, the use of the word *Millat-e-Ba'tilah* (false religious group) is in this extended meaning and, thus, it is said that *kufr* (infidelity) is *Millat-e-Wahida* (one nation).

According to Al-Munjid, the word *millat* in a religious sense connotes sharia (path), *tariqat* (doctrine) and *diat* (blood money).[9]

As per Al-Munjid, *qaum* means a group of people. *Aqwam*, *aqawim*, *aqaem* and *aqaweem* are plural forms of the word *qaum*. The *qaum* of an individual refers to the descendants (kin and kith under a single tree) of a grandfather. The word *qaum* also connotes an enemy.

The above explanations are derived from Arabic language dictionaries belonging to different ages

[9] *Al Munjid*, p. 831.

(i.e. the first, the middle and the latest in the history of the Arabic language), so that the age-old difference in the expression and meaning of the words *millat* and *qaum* becomes clear. Though, the expression and the meaning of the first age is the correct usage of the word, I have also noted its usage in the middle and the latest ages, so that no one can say that there is ample evidence in modern Arabic, Persian and Turkish languages. A person who uses the word contrary to the rule of the Arabic dictionary and grammar is wrong because the word is Arabic. Since Arabic is not the mother tongue of Iranians and Turks, their usage of this language cannot be described as authentic. Even if it is so, the fact remains that the use of this word in Arabic, especially in the Koran, is in the meaning of sharia and *deen*. How can a person who has used the Arabic word in its original sense—in the sense of its first usage and in the language of the Koran—be condemned?

What is *bulajmi* (ignorance)? Is the one ignorant who uses the words (*millat* and *qaum*) as they were in use at the time of Prophet Mohammad in Arabia, or the one who ignores the meaning of the words used during the Prophet's time and uses them in the same sense as used and understood in the modern times?

An in depth examination of this issue reveals that the ancient Arabs, Persians and Turks never used the word *millat* to denote *qaum*. Contrary to it they always used the word *millat* to denote what I have already mentioned. In the case of frequent use of a word in a text, it is sometimes omitted and a word of the same family—or a synonym—is used in its place. For instance, the word *qarya* (village) has been used thus at several places and such a practice is commonly in the Arabic language. Therefore, the claim that the word *millat* has been used in the sense of *qaum* is errnoeous. And even if this is so, it has no authenticity. If a person distorts the meaning of the word and uses it in his poetry and speech, it is his usage and understanding of the terminology. This, however, does not give him the licence to criticize others.

All these explanations of the word *qaum* reveal that the term has the following meanings in the Arabic lexicon:

1. A group of men, excluding women.
2. Primarily a group consisting of men, where women are automatically included.
3. A group comprising both men and women.

It is thus wrong to say that the word *qaum* in the lexicon does not include women, but wherever the words *qaum-e-A'ad* and *qaum-e-Moosa* appear in the Koran, they also refer to women. According to Arabic dictionaries, the word *qaum* has different connotations. Therefore, to choose a meaning from its various meanings as it is used in the Koran will not be wrong. In *Sura Hujrat* of the holy Koran, women are clearly excluded from the word *qaum*. Besides, the issue remains to be discussed that in the words *qaum-e-Moosa* and *qaum-e-A'ad*, women are automatically included or because of men. This, in my view, is the same as many imperative forms used in the Koran with words and names that are exclusively used for men, where women, too, are included.

Elucidation of the Word *Qaum* from the Glorious Koran

In order to elucidate the words *qaum* and *millat*, a close scrutiny of the holy Koran, reveals that the word *qaum* appears more than 200 times. It is not possible to discuss these in detail here. But I was accused:

How better it would have been that after passing through the pages of *Qamus* (Arabic dictionary), if not for me at least for the general Muslims, Maulana should have consulted the glorious Koran and should have examined his dangerous non-Islamic concept in the light of the revelations sent down by the Almighty Allah.

I accept that I am neither a great Islamic scholar nor a master of Arabic literature. As the saying goes:

Qalander juz do harf-e la-Ilaha Kuchh nahi rakhta
Faqih-e-shahr Qarun hai loghat ha'i hija'zi ka

A mystic possesses nothing except '*la-Ilaha*', the two words,
While a renowned scholar has the richness of the Arabic language!

I have been asked why I have relied only on the *Qamus*. Suffice it to say that I would not have ventured into the dictionary meaning, if while explaining the meaning of the word, I had not presented the explanation of the *Majma-ul-Bahar* along with the meaning given in *Qamus*. Since *Majma-ul-Bahar* also gives the same meaning as indicated in the *A'yat* (verses) of the holy Koran and the Hadith of the Prophet, its mere mention would have sufficed. Besides, my statement that search the correct meaning of these words in the verses (of the Koran) and sayings (of the Prophet) clears it further. I have said earlier that a Prophet does not invent a new language but communicates in the language that the community speaks and understands. It is sufficient for me to drive the point home by merely citing the meaning of the word as given in the Arabic dictionary.

However, since I have been asked repeatedly to explain it, I would like to say something here. In the holy Koran the word *qaum* has been used at times as a definite noun and at others as indefinite. At some places it has been used as a definite noun by affixing *alif* and *lam*. Where it has been made definite by a suffix, it points towards a proper noun. At another place it has been suffixed by a pronoun. Occasionally, it indicated the third person, or at times the second person, or even the first person. It has been used for singular, plural and also for *tasnia* (Arabic word that denotes two).

Whenever the word *qaum* has been used as indefinite or has been used with *alif* and *lam*, it clearly rules out the possibility of cooperation and unity between Muslims and non-Muslims, as being part of a nation (composite nationalism). But where the word has appeared as *muz'af* (possessive noun) and *muz'saf elaih* (pronoun), is Muslim or the Prophet, and the discussion is particularly about non-Muslims, undoubtedly at such places the word *qaum* means the inclusion of polytheists or non-Muslims with the Prophet and Muslims in composite nationalism.

For example, the verses of the holy Koran say:

'Noah's folk denied the messengers (of Allah).'
(26. 105)

'The fold of Noah denied (the truth) before them, and (so did) the dwellers at Ar-Rass and (the tribe of) Thamud. And (the tribe of) 'Aad and Pharaoh, and the brethren of Lot. And the dwellers in the wood, and the folk of Tubb'a....' (50. 12, 13, 14)

In many verses of the Koran nations have been attributed to the Prophets by the word *qaum* such as *Qaum-e-Nooh*, *Qaum-e-Ibrahim*, *Qaum-e-Lut*, *Qaum-e-Saleh* and *Qaum-e-Hud*. Similarly, sometimes, the word *qaum* has been attributed to the Prophets by using a genitive case in the third person. For example, the holy Koran says:

'We sent Noah to his people....'(71. 1)

'when he warned his folk among the wind-curved sand hills...'. (46. 21)

'And (remember) when Moses said unto his people: O' my people!...'. (61. 5)

'and whose folk are servile unto us?'(23. 47)

'There is goodly pattern for you in Abraham and those with him, when they told their folk: Lo! we are guiltless of you and all that ye worship besides Allah....' (60. 4)

Likewise, at places the personal pronoun is in reference to the second person where the Prophet is being addressed, i.e.

'And lo! It is in truth a Reminder for thee and for thy folk; and ye will be questioned.' (43. 44)

'No one of thy folk will believe save him who hath believed already....' (11. 36)

'And when the son of Mary is quoted as an example, behold! The folk laugh out.' (43. 57)

'Bring thy people forth from darkness unto light. And remind them of the days of Allah.' (14. 5)

'Appoint houses for your people in Egypt....' (10. 87)

Similarly, at times the word *qaum* has been used in the Koran as a personal pronoun and is attributed to the first person where the Prophet is indicated. The holy Koran says:

'Lo! We send Noah unto his people (saying): Warn thy people ere the painful doom come unto them. He said: O my people! Lo! I am a plain warner unto you.' (71. 12)

'O' my people! Here are my daughters! They are purer for you...' (11. 78)

'O' My people! I ask of you no reward for it....' (11. 51)

'O' my people! Bethink you, if I rely on a clear proof from my Lord....' (11. 28)

'O' my people! This is the camel of Allah, a token unto you....' (11. 64)

'O' my people! Ask forgiveness of your Lord, then turn unto Him repentant....' (11. 52)

'O' my people! Why persecute ye me, when ye well know that I am Allah's messenger....'
(61. 5)

'O' my people! Act according to your power....'
(11. 93)

Thus, there are numerous Koranic verses in which non-Muslims and the Prophet have been addressed as one nation, and infidels have been attributed to the Prophet on the basis of unity of kinship and nation. Likewise, in many Koranic verses infidels have been addressed as the nation of Muslims. In this verse, a *momin* (believer) is addressing the *pharaoh* (an infidel) as his nation:

'O' my people! Yours is the kingdom today, ye being uppermost in the land.' (40. 2)

'O' my people! Follow me. I will show you the way of right conduct.' (40. 38)

'O' my people! Lo! this life of the world is but a passing comfort, and Lo! the Hereafter, that is the enduring home.' (40. 39)

'O' my people! What aileth me that I call you unto deliverance when ye call me unto the Fire?' (40. 41)

'O' my people! Lo! I fear for you a fate like that of the factions (of old).' (40. 30)

'O' my people! Lo! I fear for a Day of Summoning.' (40. 32)

In *Sura Yasin* the Almighty Allah says:

'O' my people! Follow those who have been sent. Follow those who ask of you no fee, and who are rightly guided.' (36. 20, 21)

'We sent not down against his people after him a host from heaven, nor do We ever send.' (36. 28)

About the *Qaum-e-Moosa*, the holy Koran says in *Surah Qasas*:

'Now Korah was of Moses' folk, but he oppressed them; and We gave him so much treasure that the stores thereof would verily have been a burden for a troop of mighty men. When his own folk said tell unto him: Exult not; Lo! Allah loveth not the exultant. Then went he forth before his people in his pomp....' (28. 76, 79)

Referring to the *momin*, the holy Koran says:

'And when we inclined toward thee (Mohammad) certain of the Jinn who wished to hear the Koran and, when they were in its presence, said: Give ear! and when it was finished, turned back to their people, warning. They said: O' our people! Lo! we have heard a Scripture which hath been revealed after Moses, confirming that which was before it, guiding unto the truth and a right road. O' our people! Respond to Allah's summoner and believe in Him....' (36. 29-31)

Thus, in all the above-mentioned Koranic verses, Muslims and non-Muslims have been attributed to each other as one nation. What could this relationship be other than the country or the kinship?

The Prophet of Islam Hazrat Mohammad and other Prophets (peace be upon all of them) have been sent on earth as vice regents of Allah to establish His religion and the right code of life. The holy Koran addresses them in the following words:

'Say (O' Mohammad): O' my people! Work according to your power....' (6. 136)

In short, these verses clarify the following points:

(a) From the Koranic point of view and its usage, the word *qaum* in its essential meaning has not been used for Muslims alone—rather it is used for any group of people having the same kinship and lingual, territorial, professional ties, etc.

(b) There can be cooperation, in nationalism

and in national affairs, between a Muslim
and a non-Muslim, and many such expres-
sions and usage are seen in the holy Koran.

(c) In the sphere of national unity, a Prophet,
too, can have and has often had relationships with infidels, idol worshippers and
transgressors.

In reply to my writing, it was said:[10]

The call to follow and obey is for the reason that the
qaum (nation) is not religion and sharia, and that is
why the call and advice to hold it was useless.
Whichever group it be, whether it be of the same tribe,
of the same kinship, of even a group of bandits, of
businessmen, of residents of the city, of people belonging
to a country or geographical territory, they are merely
a group. The Almighty Allah and the Prophet do not
regard such a group of men as a rightly guided religious
community. From the point of view of the Revelation
and the Prophethood, that individual or a group of men
is not a rightly guided one. If the Revelation and the
Prophet come to them, they are the first addressees.
That is why they are attributed towards them, i.e.

---

[10] By Allama Iqbal.

Qaum-e-Nuh (the people of Noah), *Qaum-e-Lut* (the people of Lut), *Qaum-e-Musa* (the people of Moses), etc. However, if the leader of the same group is a king or a chieftain, they will be attributed towards them as well. For instance, *Qaum-e-A'ad* (the people of A'ad), *Qaum-e-Firaun* (the people of Pharaoh), etc. If two rival groups appear in a country and they belong to two opposite types of leaders, and were present in the same country led by two mutually hostile leaders, they both will be attributed to their respective leaders. For example: where there were *Qaum-e-Musa*, there were *Qaum-e-Firaun* as well.

The holy Koran says:

'The chiefs of Pharaoh's people said: (O' King), wilt thou suffer Moses and his people....' (7. 127)

However, wherever the word *qaum* appears, the group that is being reffered to is the one comprising of both believers as well as non-believers. Those who accepted the message of the Prophet were called believers and became full-fledged Muslims. It has to be remembered that infidels too have their religion and nation. As Prophet Yusuf (Joseph) says:

'I have forsaken the religion of the folk who believe not in Allah and are disbelievers in the Hereafter.' (12. 37)

This amazing passage (of Allama Iqbal) also vindicates my assertions that the word *qaum* in the holy Koran calls for national unity between believers and non-believers alike. I have been arguing it. That the term comes from the holy Koran is now accepted. To argue that infidels, too, can have their religion and nation is not surprising. I have already quoted the passage from the *Majma-ul Bahar* that says, 'The word became popular and then it was used in the meaning of false religion.' The lines that I have quoted from *Tajul Uroos* and *Sharh-e-Qamus* further clarify my views on *Muttahida Qaumiyat*. However, there still remains a vast difference between the words—*millat* and *qaum*. *Millat* means religion or sharia, or the *way of life* whether it is true or false. *Qaum* refers to men (exclusively) or a group of men and women whether they are believers or non-believers, or else provided there is a meeting point between them.

And it is for this reason that a debauch and an honourable man can be part of the same nation (*qaum*).

The following passage by Mohammad Iqbal, however, puzzles me.

A *qaum* (nation) can have their *millat* (religion), but *qaum* of *millat* have never been mentioned. This means that in the holy Koran people who belong to different nations and religions and have embraced the *Millat-e-Ibrahim* (the Religion of Abraham), thereafter they have not been called a *qaum* (nation). They have been rather addressed as *ummah*. From the use of this word (*ummah*) I had intended to explain that, as far as my knowledge goes, for Muslims in the holy Koran no other word than *ummah* has been used. If any other word has been used, kindly let me know.

Reply of
Maulana Hussain Ahmad Madani

Supposing this was the case (that no other word except *millat* has been used for Muslims in the holy Koran), it does not mean that merely no mention is proof of its negation—especially when both the *Loghvee* (dictionary) as well as the *Sharai* (religious) meaning testify to the word *millat*. Mohammad Iqbal has himself admitted rightly guided people are those who have entered into the fold of the religion (*millat*) of the Prophet. In order to authenticate my point I have quoted Jennies in the holy Koran, i.e. the *momin* of *Aal-e Firaun* (the believers among the people of Pharaoh), *momin* of *Qaum-e-Moosa* (the believers among the people of Moses), the *momin* of *Qaum-e-Isa* (the believers among the people of Jesus) and the *momineen* of Prophet Mohammad (the believers of Prophet Mohammad). When *momin* (a believer) Prophet Jesus was given the glad tidings of *jannat* (paradise) after his crucifixion, referring to the infidels as his *qaum* (nation), he says, '*Would that my people knew (what I know)*' (36. 26). The holy Koran describes the Prophets, who are believers by birth, the compatriots of non-believers. Thus (when I examine Allama Iqbal's arguments), if this discrepancy is not a wonder of the time, then what is?

While overlooking all these arguments for the time being, it is important to focus on verse of *Surah Mumtahina* in the holy Koran which reads:

'There is a goodly pattern for you in Abraham and those with him, when they told their folk: Lo! we are guiltless of you and all that ye worship beside Allah. We have done with you. And there hath arisen between us and you hostility and hate for ever until ye believe in Allah only....' (60. 4)

These are the same people who abandoned their previous religions and embraced Abraham's religion. Further, in answer to a question of Hazrat A'yesha during his last pilgrimage to Makkah, as to why Hatim (a place adjacent to Ka'ba) was separated from Ka'ba and its door heightened, the holy Prophet replied:

'Your people ran short of money (so they could not include it inside the building of Ka'ba). Were your people not close to the pre-Islamic period of ignorance, I would have demolished the Ka'ba (and would have rebuilt it on its original foundations laid by Abraham'. (Sahih Bukhari, vol. I, p. 215)

Likewise, upon the query of angels regarding the group of a faithful engaged in reciting Allah's glory, whose acts were accepted by Allah Subhanahu Wa Ta'la, whether they were serious in their prayers or were merely doing it for fun and frolic, the Almighty Allah replied:

'They are friends. So their (of *Zakirin*) friends will not be unfortunate.' (Mishka't, 197)

Thus, it is evident from the above-mentioned Koranic verses and the Hadith that the men talked about are those who have embraced Abraham's religion. But they continue to be part of the *qaum* (nation) even while being joined with others. In later traditions the word *qaum* was attributed to such Muslims only. Are the differences then not merely imaginary, poetic or philosophical?

And especially when it has been said (by Allama Iqbal):

'*Qaum* is the name of a band of men. And this band from the viewpoint of tribe, race, language, country and behaviour can appear in thousands of shades and at thousands of places.'

Earlier, too, it has been said:

'The *qaum* (nation) is not religion and sharia and that is why the call and advice to hold it firmly was useless. Whichever group it be— whether it be of the same tribe or it be of the same kinship.'

Then what is wrong if, after embracing *Millat-e-Ibrahim* (religion of Abraham), this *Millat-e-Wahidah* (single nation) is divided into different *aqwam* (nations) on the same basis that divided *Qaum-e Aus*, *Qaum-e-Khazraj*, *Qaum-e-Quraish*, *Qaum-e-Ansar*, *Qaum-e-Muhajrin*. *Qaum-e-Sufiya*, *Qaum-e Turk*, *Qaum-e-Afghan*, *Qaum-e-Kunjra* and *Qaum-e-Qasai*, etc.?

I cannot comprehend this philosophy of Allama Iqbal. As I understand and see it, due to different reasons, *millat*, too, is divided and can be divided and attributed to different *aqwam*.

A Discussion on the Word *Ummah* (Community of Believers)

Concerning the term *ummah*, it has been forcefully argued that the word denotes such people who have forsaken their nations and religions and have embraced the (true) religion of Abraham. After being proselytized, of Abraham, the word *qaum* is not used to address them.

At another place it has been said: 'As *far as I have known, for Muslims in the Holy Koran no other word than ummah has been used*. If any other word has been used, kindly let me know.' Such a statement is beyond the purview of the dictionary. The definition of the word *ummah* in the Arabic dictionary, does not include the characteristics that Allama Iqbal wants to ascribe to it.

For example, as Munjid[11] says, 'The word *ummah* connotes a group of men, ways, era, stature and so on. As per *Mukhtarus Seha*, the word *ummah* means a group of men.' According to Imam Akhfash, 'the word *ummah* is singular from the language point of view but from the point of view of meaning, it is plural. And every genus of living being is called *ummah*.' There is a saying in the Hadith compilation, 'If dogs were not a genus, I would have issued an order to kill them and that the meaning of the word *ummah* is a way and religion.'

The glorious Koran says:

'and there is not a nation but a warner hath passed among them'. (35. 24)

Another verse of the glorious Koran reads:

'And verily We have raised in every nation a messenger (proclaiming): Serve Allah and shun false gods.' (16. 36)

[11] *Al-Munjid*, p. 15.

According to yet another verse,

'And were it not that mankind would have become one community. We might well have appointed for those who disbelieved in the Beneficent, roofs of silver for their houses and stairs (of silver) whereby to mount.' (43. 33)

In short, the definition of the word *ummah* given by Allama Iqbal is of his own. Though the word *ummah* has different connotations, it does not in any way convey the sense and expression suggested by Allama Iqbal's interpretation. Rather it is used as a synonym of the word *qaum*.

Thus it is clear from the above-mentioned Koranic verses that the word *ummah* is not only used to address the group which has embraced the religion of Prophet Abraham, but the word *qaum* too has been used to address such persons.

The Word *Qaumiyat* (Nationalism) and the Discussion Related to It: Islam is a Universal Religion

All the Prophets who preceded Prophet Mohammad were sent to a particular *qaum* and a particular country, and that is why the sharia and cannon law propogated by them did not cover all the nations and the entire universe. The aim was to reform a particular community and therefore all the laws were issued accordingly. Contrary to this, Prophet Mohammad was sent for all of mankind and for the whole universe, and the corrections and reformations of all were assigned to him. The Almighty Allah says in *Surah 'A'raaf*:

'Say (O' Mohammad): O' mankind! I am the messenger of Allah to you all....' (7. 158)

'And we have not sent thee (O' Mohammad) save as a bringer of good tidings and a warner unto all mankind....' (34. 28)

'Blessed is He who hath revealed unto His slave

the criterion (of right and wrong), that he may be a warner to the people.' (25. 1)

'We sent thee not save as a mercy for the peoples.' (21. 107)

It is necessary that the rule and law that you follow not be attached to any particular *qaum*, clan or any one country, and that the message be universal so that you may call all nations and the whole universe towards your religion, and it becomes obligatory for the people to obey you. If any individual disobeys you, he is branded rebellious and is labelled a *kafir* (infidel). Such an individual is not only labelled so, but is also severely punished for his rebellion in the Hereafter. The universality of Islam means that the entire world is included in its message, and its rule is aimed at the anelioration and welfare of the whole world. Moreover, in it there are certain hidden principles and wisdom that guide and reform human beings, whether they belong to the old or new generation, whether they are white or black, or even red. It embraces the entire humanity. Despite this universality, it does not mean that the entire world will necessarily accept it.

Islam has Established Religious Unity among Its Followers

The Prophet of Islam Hazrat Mohammad has called upon the entire world to fellow the same path and the same sharia (Islamic way of life). Among those who have accepted the call and have entered its fold, Islam has established a magnificent (spiritual) bond that has overshadowed all other bonds prevalent in the world—whether based on regionalism, kinship, economics, nationalism, language and colour, caste and creed, etc. This relationship transcends the bonds of materialism and engulfs them in a spiritual body of Islamic brotherhood. To protect this bond from any harm and make it stronger, Islamic injunctions work like watering of the garden, whereby Muslims grow together like well-tended saplings. In one of his injunctions, Prophet Mohammad says:

'You will see the believers in their mutual kindness, love and sympathy just like one body. When a limb complains, the whole body responds to it with wakefulness and fever.' (Mishka't, p. 422)

According to the holy Koran,

'The believers are naught else than brothers....'
(49. 10)

A Hadith of Prophet Mohammad reads:

'A Muslim is brother to a Muslim. Neither he wrongs him, nor hands him over (to another— means enemies here).' (Mishka't, p. 422)

'Every Muslim's blood, property and honour are sacred to a Muslim.' (Mishka't, p. 422)

Islam imposes such rights and duties of a Muslim

upon its followers that differences of tribe, nation, profession, colour, caste and creed, etc., vanish. All Muslims under the sky constitute a single body and it is incumbent upon one and all (as per ability and status) to liberate a victimized Muslim living even at the farthest end of the globe. Their spiritual and temporal ruler (Caliphate) is one; their strength and honour be one too. If a former ruler accepted by the people to govern justly is illegally disposed by another, then it becomes obligatory on Muslims to behead the latter. 'If two persons simultaneously proclaimed Caliphate, kill the last one,' says the sharia.

These injunctions served to establish such a strong bond among Muslims that no power on the globe could withstand its march—neither Caesar of Rome, nor the great Persian king. Neither could the wealth of Indian princely states remain intact, nor the brave Turk emperors. Wherever any power attacked Muslims, Islamic forces would rush to their aid and the enemies were overpowered. This pan-Islamism elevated Islam above all religions, nations and countries.

There is no doubt that as per the call and its power of absorption, Islam and its concept of *qaumiyat* are based on *sharfe insani* (human dignity) and *ikhwate bashri* (human brotherhood). It is this that makes it universal. However, as far as co-ordination, right to kindred and affection, eternal friendship, unity and everlasting cooperation are concerned, they have been reserved for believers and those who have embraced Islam, irrespective of their race.

The statement of the editor of *Ehsaan* that 'instead of geographical boundary and racial unity, the concept of Islamic nationalism is based on human dignity and human brotherhood cannot be correct from any perspective. Otherwise, it is likely that every individual and the entire population, whether Jew or Christian, Hindu or Muslim, Sikh or Zoroastrian, Buddhist or Jain, Black or White, Asian or African, would become a nation because they, too, have human dignity and feelings of universal brotherhood. They all are the children of Adam. As the holy Koran says:

'Surely We created man of the best stature....'
(95. 4)

And again:

'We have honoured the sons of Adam provided them with transport on land and sea giving them for sustenance things good and pure and conferred on them special favour above a great part of our creation'. (15.70)

As far my knowledge goes, I have not come across any Koranic verse or saying of Prophet Mohammad that points to human dignity and human brotherhood as a basis of nationalism. It was for this reason that I had asked the editor of *Ehsaan* to substantiate his claim by citing a verse from the holy Koran. Unfortunately, he failed to cite a single Koranic verse or Hadith to substantiate his claim that Islam holds that the basis of nationalism can only be humanism and universal brotherhood. According to this criterion, all those individuals who advocate humanism should be considered as one nation.

Certain complexities of philosophical arguments create confusion:

Nobody should get confused by words like human dignity. In Islamic studies such words signify to the sublime truth that has been entrusted to the human heart and soul. That is to say, the almanac of man is from the nature of Allah, and ungratefulness, that is discontinuity, is dependent upon the passion that is running in the veins of man for the unity of Allah. If we look at the history of man, we find a constant chain of reciprocity.

I am not prepared to either certify or condemn these expressed truths and imaginations. I have only one demand from which verse of the Koran or saying of the Prophet are human dignity and human brotherhood derived as a basis for *qaumiyat*? In other words, only those men who advocate universal brotherhood are to be considered as a single nation and not the people of one country, one race or one colour.

'If my statement is against the Islamic faith, Maulana (Hussain Ahmad Madani) may correct (and say) Islam does not give the message of human dignity and universal brotherhood. It rather makes the children of Adam, Indian...,' writes the editor of the Urdu daily *Ehsaan*. What were the claims and what is being stated? I have already elaborated on the message of Islam has brought and the unity it demands.

Policy of the Enemies of Islam

The spirit of kinship, unity, coordination and cooperation that the teaching of the founder of Islam Prophet Muhammad infused in the Muslim *qaum* left the enemies of Islam at their wits' end. They tried their utmost to crush the spirit of pan-Islamism among Muslims, knowing fully well that this was the only way to protect themselves from the global onslaught of Muslims. Besides, they were well aware that only in this way they could overpower the Muslim nation.

The enemies of Islam in every age have attempted this and have more or less succeeded. Exhausted by the relentless attacks by Turks of the

Khilafate Uthmaniya, and the solidarity and unified stand of the Muslim nation, Europe launched a systematic and well-orchestrated plan against pan-Islamism. This plan bore fruit after a century of struggle by producing two types of spirit among Muslims. The first is racial, nationalistic and linguistic divisions and differences. The second is the approach and thinking that *jihad* (holy war) should not be for religious and spiritual purposes, but for race and country, so as to divorce the religious spirit from it.

The successful plan of Europeans on these two fronts arrested the march of the Ottoman Caliphate that had trampled upon country after country in Europe. European efforts not only weakened the spirit of Islam and reduced the Ottoman to a termite infested piece of wood, but it also created disenchantment among Turks with the spirit of the Caliphate. Romania, Bulgaria, Bosnia Herzegovina, Greece, Albania and Croatia broke away from the Ottoman Empire on racial, cultural, lingual and national grounds. Not only was the Christian populace separated, but also efforts were made to drive a wedge between Muslim nations and Turks. It was due to this that Arabs and Kurds were distanced from Turkey. It is difficult to recount in words how European nations brutalized and suppressed the peoples of Iraq, Syria, Palestine, Cyprus and Arabia after driving a wedge between them and Turkey.

At this critical juncture of history no Muslim preacher came to the fore to teach Muslims the meaning of composite nationalism and patriotism, race and language, etc. Nor did any one rise to challenge the onslaught of Europeans in the fields of academics and communications. As a result, pan-Islamism became a fable of the past and Muslim countries became prey to the Europeans.

Aversion to Composite Nationalism and Patriotism

When the fabric of Muslim unity in Asia, Europe and Africa has been shredded to pieces, we are told that Islam preached only Muslim unity, and that it can neither unite with non-Muslims nor can it forge composite nationalism with them. If a Muslim joins a non-Muslim on the basis of nationalism or race or profession and forges a sort of unity, he is branded as an enemy of Islamic teachings, 'nationalism', 'secularism', etc., which Islam does not permit and which are the negation of the Koranic teachings. The same story was repeated in the case of handicrafts and commerce which were once thriving and Indian products were dominating the markets in England and in other European countries. At the same time the philosophy of 'safe and secure trade' was propogated by Europeans and every newspaper, journal and intellectual's lecture sang paeans of its virtues as if it was a source of eternal bliss for mankind. However, when the Indian economy and commerce were weakened by this policy and 'made in England' goods began to dominate the market, the philosophy of 'free trade' was preached to us. We were told that the philosophy of 'safe and secure trade' had proven wrong.

As a result, the handicraft industry of India was

completely destroyed. When the Muslims were dominant, the West harangued the philosophy that European map could not be changed and that the victorious nation could not annex the territory of the vanquished country. However, when the Muslim power was weakened, the European philosophy underwent a dramatic change. A new philosophy was propounded that the victors could not be denied access to their booty.

How dangerous the formation of any outfit based on the principles of composite nationalism was for the British can be gauged from the statement of Professor Selley. In his article the Professor opined that

if this spirit was infused in the hearts of Indian people, though it may not be strong to overthrow the mighty British, it would be enough to enliven the spirit that any cooperation with a foreign power would be a shameful act. This would eventually lend to the downfall of British rule.

Thus, the nationalism that the West did not tire of praising remained endearing and praiseworthy so long as Islam and the rule of Islamic

Caliphate were dominant. After the defeat of Muslim power, however, the same nationalism became despicable. Indeed, this is strange!

Curse of Nationalism

If nationalism is so abhorrent, and since Europe used it as an effective weapon to destroy the Ottoman Empire, Muslims too, should have used it to undermine the power of the British. It would have been a case of using the same weapon to destroy the enemy that the enemy had used against Muslims. Indian Muslims should have adopted it to seek revenge on their enemy.

However, this did not happen. Knowingly or unknowingly, the philosophy is being taught to Indian Muslims that nationalism is to be abhorred. The establishment of any unity based on composite nationalism with non-Muslims is religiously impermissible as well as harmful for the Islamic cause. The Muslim community was a miniscule minority but did not get absorbed in the mainstream for centuries. Today, when their population has crossed 80 million, it is argued that they would become a morsel for the Hindus.

Islamic Brotherhood

Undoubtedly, as I have mentioned earlier, the Prophet of Islam Hazrat Mohammad created a bond among Muslims that is superior to all bonds. In comparison, bonds such as nationalism are pale and colourless. A Muslim, whoever and wherever he is, is the brother of another Muslim and he has right over other Muslims. This bond of *rabita* (relationships) exists only among those who have accepted Islam. In the case of those who have not embraced Islam, this bond cannot be established. They could be part of composite nationalism, but only through the bonds of *nasal* (race), *rang* (colour) and nationality, etc.

The question is: Can a Muslim join hands with non-Muslims and become part of the same nation and on the basis of this composite nationalism, can he enter into *siyasate mulki* and forge economic, commercial, agricultural and industrial relations with them? Is there a need of such a thing in India?

It is quite apparent that waiting for all Indians to become Muslims in order to enter into such an alliance is wrong and harmful. There is no doubt that Islam combines principles of both ideological and practical reformation. Moreover, it does not only strive for the reformation of an individual, but also strives to reform society as a whole—irrespective of privileged or under-privileged. Islam focuses on problems universally and permits all sorts of reforms. But the point is whether Islam (the Islamic principles that deal with individual as well as community life and pertain to such issues as God, relationship of God with His creatures and relationship between His creatures) permits that together with non-Muslims, a United Front can be formed on the basis of *wataniyat, nasal, rang* or language (*zabaan*), etc., to defeat the enemies of Islam and benefit Muslims in political, commercial, agricultural and industrial fields, without compromising on the basic tenets of Islam?

As far as I have studied and followed the verses of the holy Koran, I have understood that there is no clear cut categorization of it, i.e. at times it is obligatory, at other times it is desirable, or preferable, or permissible, or even prohibited. Its condemnation is only on the basis that nationalism, in Western parlance today, is applied to those principles that relate to collective human life and that is altogether anti-religion, and thus would be attributed by this particular terminology. However, this meaning of nationalism is neither popular among people, nor would a true Muslim accept it, nor is there any such movement underway. Neither the Indian National Congress and its volunteers are propagating it. Therefore, raking up this issue to an emotional pitch is an exercise in futility.

It must be remembered that we form a united body everyday to achieve our common goal. Not only do we participate in it, but we also often struggle to acquire its membership and spend thousands of rupees for this. While defining such a membership as beneficial for the nation and community, we consider our participation obligatory. Town area, unified area, municipal board, district board, councils, assemblies and educational institutions and hundreds of such organizations and associations are formed with a definite purpose on the same principle of law and with the intention to serve the common interest. Interestingly, participation in such *anjuman* (association) is not prohibited.

However, and strangely enough, when the same type of association is formed for the liberty of the country from British occupation, it is declared *haram* (prohibited) against Islamic teachings, against our soul and our conscience, and even against common sense. When a nationalist outfit is formed on the basis of the principle of composite nationalism, why is it viewed as illegal? When an issue arises in councils and assemblies against a fundamental principle of Islam, it is rejected. The same will happen in a set up that is based on the principle of composite nationalism.

Action Plan for India

All individuals and communities living in India have many things in common that have been violated by the foreign rulers for its vested inetersts. It has not only made their lives miserable, but has also pushed them to the verge of extinction. Since Indians are suffering because they have lost sight of their common interests, they need to struggle to regain their lost rights. It is incumbent on them to make a united effort to throw off the yoke of foreign slavery and open avenues for the progress of the citizens of India. The objective is to establish composite nationalism on the basis of national unity. The life of Prophet Mohammad to achieve such an objective through the formation of a United Front with non-Muslims.

The United Front that Prophet Mohammad Formed of Muslims and Non-Muslims

After fourteen years of prophethood in Madina, Hazrat Mohammad along with his companions from Quraish and Ansar on the one hand, as well as the resident Jews of Madina on the other, formed a United Front based on a comprehensive written agreement that brought them together as one nation against their common enemy. They, however, professed and adhered to their respective religions.

In his Presidential address at the conference of Jamiat,[12] the late Maulana Anwar Shah Kashmiri refers to and quotes from this historical event:

Although in this brief address I cannot shed light on all the aspects of *Darul Aman* (land of peace—Madina), yet it is important here to highlight certain relevant points. And for this it is necessary to draw your attention toward those clauses of the agreement amongst Jews and Muslims of Madina that Prophet Mohammad made in his early period of migration to that city. It is (quite clear) that Muslims in *Darul Aman* (land of peace) and *Darul Harb* (land of war) can make agreement with a non-Muslim nation, viz., the Agreement of Mohammad Rasulallah with Jews of Madina. Since the contents of the agreement are

---

[12] Three-day conference of Jamiat Ulama-i-Hind held at Peshawar on 2–4 December 1927.

lengthy and I see no need of copying the Arabic text, I present here only relevant articles of the agreement.

In the name Allah, most gracious, most merciful

This is an agreement from Mohammad, the Messenger of Allah, which will be enforceable amongst Muslim Quraish, Muslims of Madina and other residents who have participated in wars, agreed upon and become ally.

Article 1

All parties to the covenant (*quraish, mohajir, ansar* and Jew) shall be regarded as one nation against other non-Muslim and non-signatory parties.

Article 8

It is incumbent upon Muslims to help and have sympathetic attitude towards Jews who are party to the covenant. Neither they (Jews) shall be subjected to any wrongdoings, nor any atrocity against them shall be abetted.

Article 15

Bani Auf (a tribe of Jews) is a party to the agreement and *haleef* (ally) of Muslims. Jews shall be free to practice their religion, so shall be Muslims. Apart from the religion, in other community affairs Muslims and Bani Auf shall be regarded as *ek quam* (one nation). Any one committing atrocity and breach of agreement or any wrongdoing shall be liable for punishment.

Prophet Mohammad thereafter mentioned other Jewish tribes, viz., Bani Najjar, Bani Haarith, Bani Saida, Bani Jasham and Bani Al-Aus and clarified that since these Jewish tribes, too, had accepted and become party to the agreement, they shall have the same rights and privileges as that of Bani Auf.[13]

[13] Excerpts from pp. 21, 23 and 25.

It is reported from *Ibne Ishaque* that Prophet Mohammad got a covenant signed between Mohajrin (emigrants from Makkah) and Ansar (helpers of Madina) in which Jews too were included, and they were left free to practice their religion and possess property. He imposed certain conditions upon Jews and accepted certain conditions put forth by them.[14]

In the name of Allah, most gracious, most merciful

This is an agreement of Mohammad, the Prophet of Allah, signed between his companions, Muslims of Quraish tribe, Muslims of Madina, those under their allegiance, those who join them and those who shall fight against their enemies shoulder to shoulder with them.

Jews along with Muslims shall bear the expenses (of war) till Muslims are engaged in war and Bani Auf (a Jewish tribe) and Muslims shall be an *ummah*. Jews shall practice their religion and Muslims their own—every individual, slaves, the liberated ones as well as their masters. However, the one who commits a wrong and is guilty of committing a crime, he shall only cause to perish his life and the life of his household. Jews of Bani Najjar tribe shall have the rights that Jews of Bani Auf have. Jews of Bani Saida shall have the same rights that Jews of Bani Auf have, and those of Bani Jasham,

[14] Seerah Ibn-e-Hisham, vol. 1, p. 278.

Bani Al-Aus and Banu Shoaib shall have the same rights that Bani Auf have. But whosoever commits a wrong and is guilty of committing a crime, he shall cause to perish only himself and the members of his household.

Abu Obaida Bin Qasim Al Azwi writes the following in his book entitled *Kitab-ul-Amwal:*[15]

This declaration is of the Prophet of Allah, agreed upon between the residents of the city of Madina and the Quraish and for all those who supported them and sided with them and fought wars on their side that, with exception, as against other party they are but one *ummah.*

This declaration of a bond is fairly lengthy in which Muslim tribes of 'migrants' and 'helpers' have been mentioned and the description is of different Jewish tribes and the existing agreements between each of them. The author writes:

...And Muslims, leaving others, shall help each other. And whoever from among Jews shall support us, it is

[15] Abu Obaida Bin Qasim Al Azwi died in the Hijri year 48. This quote is from his book entitled *Kitab-ul-Amwal,* p. 402.

for their well being, they shall not be wronged'. (p. 203)

He further added:

...During the war period, Jews shall bear the expenses of war with the Muslims and Jews of Bani Auf, and their helpers shall be considered as an *ummah* of Ansar (the helpers). Jews shall follow their religion and Muslims shall follow their own. But whosoever commits a wrong and is guilty of committing a crime, he shall cause none to perish but only himself and the members of his household. And Bani Najjar too shall have the rights that the Jews of Bani Auf have. (p. 204)

Many Jewish tribes have been mentioned by name thereafter and also the terms and conditions of the covenant. The covenant itself and its provisions have been mentioned and discussed in many books. In the chapter of Prophets, he writes:

In the name of Allah, most gracious, most merciful

This agreement is from Mohammad, the Prophet of Allah, between and amongst the Muslims, Quraish of Makkah and the residents of Madina and with those who followed, supported and took part in *Jihad* with them with this confession and contract that they are one *ummah* against their enemies. (p. 230)

Further, he says,

...And with this condition that Jews shall bear the cost
of war equally with the Muslims till the latter is in war
and with this condition that Jews of Bani Auf (tribe)
shall be regarded as a group of Muslims. Jews shall follow
their religion and Muslims shall follow theirs. (p. 232)

The gist of my argument is that the Prophet
brought together Muslims and Jews into one
'nation' to fight against the enemies. Under this
covenant to fight a war, certain conditions of
non-Muslims (Jews) were accepted and certain
conditions were imposed. Moreover, in the
covenant the word *ummah* (followers) was used
instead of *qaum* (nation), and it said that Muslims
and Jews should be considered as one nation as
against those who were not included in the
covenant. Although Allama Iqbal considers the
word *ummah* as superior to the word *qaum*, the
word *ummah* is used only to denote Muslims. This
word, according to him, denotes only those people
who have renounced their former religions and
embraced the religion of Abraham. Further, apart

from the word *ummah* no other word is used to denote Muslims.

The pertinent issue is: if Muslims cannot form a nation with non-Muslims, if Islam does not permit it and if Islam does not have the flexibility to form in any condition a composite nationalism on the basis of race and region, then how was it that the Prophet formed a composite *ummah* with the Jews? And how did the Jews and Muslims became one *ummah* according to the covenant of the Prophet as against other *aqwam*? Over and above this, it was clearly mentioned in the covenant that the Muslims and the Jews would be free to pursue their respective religions. And while calling them one *ummah* the word '*minal momineen*' (from believers) was used. This proves that *muttahida qaum* (a nation united) irrespective of people being free to pursue their different religions is possible, and that they too can be considered Muslim *ummah*.

From what has been described above, it becomes apparent that for Muslims to become a nation or to form a nation with non-Muslims is neither undue interference in religious affairs nor it is against the spirit of common welfare that Islamic law envisages. A Muslim while observing his religion can join hands with non-Muslims and can become a nation as they have lived earlier. Islam is a flexible religion—especially at a time when it is at war and there is need to acquire more power and strength to defeat the enemy.

Islam is a Flexible Religion

To think and argue that Islam is not a flexible religion is something that I cannot really understand. As far as I have delved into the principles of Islamic jurisprudence, it can coexist peacefully with non-Muslims. Islam can have a covenant with non-Muslims, it permits commerce with them, joint ownership of properties and borrowing and lending with them.

Muslims can also live and interact with non-Muslims. They can share in their happiness and sorrows. They can drink water from the same tap and eat in the same plate. Muslims are permitted to visit the land of infidels and the country at war and settle there. They can marry the daughters of their avowed enemies, the Jews and the Christians. They can eat meat of animals slaughtered by them, provided they are slaughtered in the name of Allah. They consider the life and the property of their subjects equally inviolable as their own. There are innumerable principles and laws in Islam that emphasize kindness, magnanimity, tolerance, etc., these are cardinal principles on which a common body is formed. In fact, this is the criticism that Catholic Christians have always levelled against Islam—that it grants equal religious liberty to its subjects as well as to its followers.

Islam is not fanatical and discriminatory like Hinduism, that considers the followers of all other religions as *mlecchas* (untouchables) and food touched by them as inedible. In Hinduism a section of people of its *qaum* is labelled *shudra* (untouchable). It has no place for those who have left its fold.

Islam is more liberal than Judaism. The latter considers the consumption of meat of an animal that has been slaughtered by a non-Jew as not fit for consumption. Also, it prohibits the entry of the other nations of the world into its fold. Neither is Islam insensitive like Buddhism which has no specific principles by which its followers could claim to have a distinct identity.

Islam is known for its true principles of individual and collective life that it offers to human beings. It operates at two levels—one deals with the Creator of the universe and the second deals with His created beings—whether it is related to the ideology, behaviour and action of an individual or to the collective life of the common people or elite. Islam is a tolerant and a forward-looking religion that calls the whole world towards itself and is also ready to tolerate all the religions of the world. While being aware of the truth of their falsehood, it is ready to mingle with them; co-exist with them and even establish reciprocal ties with them.

In fact, this is the meaning of its flexibility. Flexibility does not denote weakness or giving credence to falsehood, illegitimate behaviour and immoral deeds.

Ordained Meaning of
Composite Nationalism

By composite nationalism I mean here 'nation-alism', the foundation of which was laid down by Prophet Mohammad in Madina. That is to say, the people of India as Indians, as a nation united (despite religious and cultural diversity), should become one solid nation and should wage war against the alien power that has usurped their natural rights. It is incumbent upon every Indian to fight against such a barbaric regime and throw off the shackles of slavery. It is important not to interfere in another's religion—rather all nations (communities) living in India are free to practice their religion, live by its moral values and act according to their religious traditions. While maintaining peace and tranquillity, they should propagate their ideology, follow their culture, promote civilization and protect their personal law. Neither should a minority interfere in the personal affairs of other minorities or the majority, nor should the majority strive to assimilate the minority into itself.

This is what the Indian National Congress has been striving to achieve ever since its inception. In its first session in 1885, it outlined its main objectives in the following words: 'To unite the divergent and conflicting elements—that form the Indian populace—and turn them into one nation.'[16]

However, even after this (somewhat ambiguous) declaration, it has always stated that all citizens shall be free to pursue their religion, culture, personal law, etc. The proposal discussed at the meeting of the All India Congress Committee meeting on 8 August 1931, described the fundamental rights and duties of the citizens:

Any constitutional provision or declaration that the Indian National Congress would make or through it the Independent Government shall make, it essentially shall have the following points:

(1) Every Indian citizen shall have the following rights,

---

[16] Raushan Mustaqbil, p. 281.

i.e. freedom of speech and expression, total freedom of coordinated action and collaboration and right to peaceful, without arms, assembly for any purpose that is neither immoral nor against the law.

(2) Every Indian citizen shall have the freedom of conscience and right to declare, follow and propagate his religion—provided it does not degenerate and causes public disorder.

(3) All religious minorities shall have the constitutional right to protection of their cultures, languages and their religious rituals. Besides, the areas inhabited by linguistic minorities shall have adequate safeguard to their languages.

The Working Committee meeting of the Indian National Congress, held in Calcutta on 26 October 1937, reinforced and elaborated the same objectives.

Rights of Minorities

The Indian National Congress has consistently said that it considers its duty to protect minorities, safeguard their cultural, political and economic rights and provide full opportunity for their growth in these fields. The main objective of the Indian National Congress is to liberate India and create unity among peoples of all faiths whereby the entire nation would work for the progress of India, without harming others for its partisan end. From liberation and cooperation it should not be construed that from among different cultures and civilizations a particular culture shall be singled out and subjected to pressures—rather it will be protected so that all the communities feel free to follow their traditions and progress without any hindrance. Since there have been efforts to create confusion among people towards the policy of the Congress, the All India Congress Committee once again would like to reaffirm and declare its policy. As for the rights of minorities, the following principles are put forth:

(1) Every citizen of India shall be free to express his opinion, form a society and organization and shall have the right to peaceful, without arms, assembly for any such purpose that is neither immoral nor against the law.

(2) Every citizen shall be free to profess his religious views and also shall be free to join any religious group—provided it does not degenerate and cause public disorder.

(3) Language, culture and script of all religious and

linguistic minorities residing in different provinces shall be protected.

(4) Irrespective of religion, caste and gender, all shall be equal before the law.

(5) There shall be no differentiation on the basis of religion, caste and gender in employment for any ordinary government post or that of responsibility and dignity.

(6) All citizens shall have equal rights and duties in using public facilities such as roads, schools, ponds and other facilities built by government funds for the welfare of the general public.

(7) The government shall maintain neutrality and impartiality in discharging its duties.

The above articles concerning the basic rights of minorities make it abundantly clear that there shall be no interference in the religious and cultural affairs of minorities, and they will retain their 'personal law' given to them in the Constitution. The majority cannot and shall not pressurize the minority for any changes in their personal law.[17]

[17] Congress party Bulletin, published by the All India Congress Committee, dated 2 December 1937, pp. 10–12.

Later, the Congress party in its General Body meeting[18] held at Haripura, Surat district on 19–21 February 1938, declared the same in the following words and approved all previous resolutions passed by the All India Congress Committee.

The Indian National Congress welcomes the sentiments and spirit of Muslims and other minorities in the fight against the colonial and imperialist power. It also welcomes united participation of all sections and communities in India's freedom struggle that is same for one and all. The Congress specially welcomes the large number of the minority community (Muslims) who have joined the Indian National Congress and strengthened its hand in the liberation struggle against the oppressive foreign power.

The resolution pertaining to minorities' rights that was prepared by the Working Committee at Calcutta in October 1937, this (General Body Meeting) session endorses, approves and also reaffirms that it is the foremost duty and basic policy of the Congress to protect the religious, linguistic and cultural rights of

[18] General Body Meeting of the Congress held at Haripura, Surat district, on 19–21 February 1938.

minorities. In the government's schemes where there is the Congress party's involvement, minorities shall be encouraged to prosper, progress and participate in their cultural, political and economic affairs.

These declarations of the Indian National Congress make it abundantly clear that it was in favour of the formation of composite nationalism in India and v'as opposed to undue interference in the religious, cultural, linguistic and personal affairs of Indian citizens. It was only concerned with issues of common needs and interests that had been usurped by an alien government and used to destroy the interests of the common people.

These affairs are more or less similar to those required for participation in public forums like town area, notified area, municipal boards, district boards, councils and assemblies. This is not implemented with a view to absorb a nation or a religion into another nation and religion. Though the rules and regulations of these institutions vary, there is neither salvation in it for Indian citizens nor can participation in it be equated with atheism, irreligiousness, disbelief and assimilation in another religion. Also, it is possible to refrain from participating in these institutions because of such fears.

An examination of Islamic teachings and the earliest history of Islam reveals that the foundation of composite nationalism can be traced from the life of Prophet Mohammad. His life clearly shows that the composite nationalism that he formed of non-Muslim nations, while remaining free in spheres of religion and sharia (religious code), shall be regarded one *qaum* and one *ummah* in events such as war and commerce.

A study of the Muslim period and recent events, indicates that innumerable associations were formed between Muslims and non-Muslims. These associations were based on a common point of absorption between them—whether it was regional affiliation or national affiliation or business affiliation or professional associations such as education, military, industry and politics. The struggle and coming together of both communities in such organizations is neither regarded as an irreligious act nor anti-national, nor is any fear of affiliation with atheism rational, nor is the fear of assimilation and absorption justified.

Fear of European Nationalism and Patriotism

It is possible that Europeans have used nationalism and patriotism in a different sense: to create a different but definite social milieu. Perhaps after realizing their purpose and objective are in contravention to the objectives of their religious establishments, they have altogether abandoned religion or have assigned it to the personal domain of an individual. Is it necessary that our efforts towards composite nationalism or patriotism be guided by the same social milieu that existed in Europe? On the basis of this should a verdict be given that since the meaning of composite nationalism or patriotism in Europe is in contravention to Islam, it should be prohibited altogether?

Who does not know that in modern democracy Europe has adopted many practices and priciples that are either not found in the Islamic teachings or are directly opposed to it. In this case should a *fatwa* (religious edict) be issued that to establish democracy or to speak in its favour and support is not permissible—though its foundation was laid down by Islam?

Who is not aware that Europe has enacted certain collective laws for business and industrial establishments and companies, many clauses of which are in total contravention to the principles of Islamic law. Should a *fatwa* be issued that to set up business establishments, companies or industries, and many such associations for the armed forces and the agricultural sector is illegal?

It must be accepted that forming associations is not only essential, but is also right. However, it is important to eschew those things that are in contravention to Islamic teachings. The same principle has to be followed while forming any national or political association. If any board—whether it is at the district level or the state level, whether it is the Bar Association or the Educational Association—adopts a clause that is against Islam, it is the moral duty of Muslims to oppose and struggle against it.

Composite nationalism of Indian citizens aims to intice in them the spirit of national unity and freedom so that they can liberate themselves from the clutches of an oppressive foreign power. A foreign power that has plundered their treasure, wealth and happiness; destroyed the fabric of their religion, tradition, culture, art and craft; demolished their language and education system; trampled upon their honour and pride; demolished their self-respect and courage, and eroded their unity, love and human traits. An imposed government that has irreparably damaged each and every religion and culture on the Indian soil, especially Muslims whom it has relegated to the lowest rung through its cunning diplomacy.

In the prevailing situation, only nationalism can generate the power of gravitation among people of different religions in India. To produce this power of gravitation, composite nationalism is very essential so that all *aqwam* (different religious groups) living in India join hands and wage a war of freedom, standing shoulder to shoulder with each other, in order to usher in peace and prosperity in the country. There is no other way to protect our religion and culture from the British onslaught. It is this united action that is intended by the term composite nationalism. It is not intended to convey what my adversaries have interpreted that (would mean) after jettisoning Islam one should come under such system that is synonymous with atheism and agnosticism.

The Real Danger

There are fears that close proximity with non-Muslims, concentration on organizational and defence issues and daily contacts in political affairs will lead Muslims away from their religion. Further, the cultural identity of all nation will gradually be lost at the hands of agnosticism. Such fears are unwarranted. This could only happen when there is no conviction towards the religion and the sense of its protection. The protection of religion is necessary and that is why resolutions protecting the religious identity of Muslims have been passed by the Congress from time to time.

Moreover, these things have occurred and can also occur due to interactions in the field of politics, economics and other worldly affairs. In fact, English education imparted in schools, colleges and universities is the biggest source of it. Almost 80 to 90 per cent of Muslims graduating from these educational institutions are irreligious and apostate. Their appearance, their dress, their thinking, even their deeds and their character are not like Muslim. Those who wax eloquent about Islam and religion, do not differ in their dress and appearance from the British. And why should they? Lord Macaulay had said:

We must at present do our best to form a class who may be interpreters between us and the millions whom we govern [...] a class of persons Indians in blood and colour, but English in tastes, in opinions, in moral and in intellect.[19]

[19] *The Great Indian Education Debate*, edited by Lynn Zastoupil and Martin Moir, p. 171.

Should a *fatwa* be issued then that English education, English colleges and universities should be closed down and that Muslims should not enrol in them, especially when we have already witnessed their adverse impact?

The danger of composite nationalism in India, if any, remains in the realm of experiment. Moreover, the situation that exists in Europe cannot be a parameter for us in India. Europeans are hardcore materialists. Where is religion in their lives? And if there was once, what was its intensity, its level? Besides, in a true sense, they never had any religious leadership which could have protected the religious tradition and chalked out a course along the religious lines.

The new upsurge in the poisonous current of atheism and agnosticism among Indian youths and in the educated class of Muslims is the result of constant intermingling with the British and the effect of their education and their rule. This is happening even though the British government has not passed any ordinance and law enforcing them, and they remain a tiny minority in this country. Nevertheless, the zeal for imitation of the British culture and tradition among the common people and especially among Muslim youth, has increasingly alienated them from Islam—to the extent of hatred. To blame composite nationalism for this situation would be a grave mistake. Had this been the case, Prophet Mohammad would have never supported it.

The lack of religious knowledge coupled with lack of faith and belief compel the people to bow before a false religion and tradition. Having lived for more or less a thousand years under Muslim rule, Hindus of Delhi and United Provinces did not forsake their 'Choti-Dhoti' culture. Muslims residing in these areas could not progress beyond 16 per cent. The reason cannot be anything but the Hindu's firm belief in their religion.

In spite of Muslims being in a majority in countries like Egypt and despite of their being a non-aligned nation, the influence of atheism and agnosticism is increasing. On the contrary, even in far-flung areas in India, Indian Muslims have safeguarded their religiosity than the Egyptian and

Syrian Muslims. Can the credit for this be given to any thing other than the earnestness of its adherents and their efforts to devise means to protect it?

In other words, to define composite nationalism as a source of atheism and agnosticism—especially with all these safeguards—would be erroneous. As far as mixing with any thing other than religion is concerned, it undoubtedly leads to impiety and irreligiousness.

Interaction of the Islamic System with Other Systems

The assumption that Islam and its adherents cannot confederate and interact with any other system is unacceptable. Although Islamic jurisprudence and sharia contains written views on several matters, there remain uncountable things that are allowed, and in which each person is free to act upon as per his expediency. Among these are kingdoms, their ordinances and organizations, etc., that are used as ways and means of expediency. If certain resolutions are mooted by an agricultural or a commercial or an industrial establishment and practical action is taken to implement them, being Islamic, our participation would not be illegal from any point of view. There are many collective ordinances in the sharia that are based on Islamic rule. These do not address the individual, but Caliphs and Sultans. When there is no Islamic government, it is neither obligatory nor permissible that an individual or a unit of Muslims act upon it. In such a situation the duty of the unit shall be only that as per its capabilities it should strive to establish an Islamic government. Penal ordinances and capital punishments fall under this category. Before this, it would be permissible and desirable that Muslims take action and try to implement those ordinances that are closer to the national interest and beneficial to the community. Thus, how can it be expedient and correct to pronounce illegal the unity and cooperation with other (non-Islamic) collective bodies on the basis of the collective laws of Islam?

It is Possible for an Individual and a Nation to have Different Identities

An individual can at the same time be a member of different organizations, the duties and responsibilities of which may vary in accordance with his assignments and posts. For example, an individual can be a son, a father, a son-in-law, a father-in-law, a disciple, a mentor and a ruler, and can discharge the duties of each role accordingly. He can also be a member of different parties and organizations at the same time, and strictly follow their rules and regulations. It is equally possible that an individual is a member of the bar association, of the municipal board, assembly or parliament and at the same time be a member of a trade union, an education board, and fruitfully discharge all his duties. Similarly, it is possible that a person is attached to one or more non-Muslim organizations on the basis of kinship or profession or nation, and shares composite nationalism with them and at the same time he champions the unity of Muslim *ummah* all over the world. And thus, as per his agreement with those organizations and as per the teachings of the religion, discharges his assigned duties. A verse of the holy Koran reads:

'. . . but if they seek help from you in the matter of religion then it is your duty to help (them) except against a folk between whom and you there is a treaty. . . .' (8. 72)

This Koranic verse makes it amply clear that a Muslim being part of the *ummah* can also maintain a relationship with non-Muslims. While assisting and cooperating with his Muslim brothers, he can abide by the clauses of the agreement that he has entered into with non-Muslims. In the event that a clause of the agreement that a Muslim has entered into with non-Muslims goes against the interest of the Muslim *ummah*, he would perforce abide by the clause of the agreement and withdraw all assistance and cooperation to Muslims.

While living in India and forming a *qaum* with other communities in the country, Muslims can retain their Muslimness and can also protect their rights, distinct culture, language, religion and personal law, and can also think and act for their protection. While discharging their national duty, they can maintain their relationship with the Muslim *ummah* whether they live in Afghanistan, Iran, Iraq, Hejaz, Yemen, Syria, Palestine, Egypt, Asia Minor, West Asia, Africa, Europe, and America, etc. There is no inherent contradiction between the two. This neither affects the universal Islamic affinity of Indian Muslims nor there can be a clash with the universal Islamic affinity of Muslims living in other countries.

While delivering his last speech at the Round Table Conference in London on 12 September 1932, Maulana Mohammad Ali Jauhar said:

One word as to the Muslim position, with which I shall deal at length on some other occasion. Many people in England ask us why this question of Hindu and Muslim comes into politics, and what it has to do with these things. I reply, it is a wrong conception of religion that you have, if you exclude politics from it. It is not dogma; it is not ritual! Religion, to my mind, means the interpretation of life. I have a culture, a polity, an outlook on life—a complete synthesis which is Islam. Where God commands I am a Muslim first, a Muslim second, and a Muslim last, and nothing but a Muslim. If you ask me to enter into your Empire or into your nation by leaving that synthesis, that polity, that culture, that ethics, I will not do it. My first duty is to my maker, not to H.M. the King, nor to my companion Dr. Moonje; my first duty is to my maker, and that is the case with Dr. Moonje; also. He must be a Hindu first, and I must be a Muslim first, so far as that duty is concerned. But where India is concerned, where India's freedom is concerned, I am an Indian first, an Indian second, an Indian last, and nothing but an Indian.

I belong to two circles of equal size, but which are not concentric. One is India, and the other is Muslim world. When I came to England in 1920 at the head of the Khilafat Delegation, my friend said: 'You must have some sort of a crest for your stationary.' I decided to have it with two circles on it. In one circle was the word 'India'; in the other circle was Islam, with the word 'Khilafat'. We as Indian Muslims came in both circles. We belong to these two circles, each of more than 300 millions, and we can leave neither. (This estimation is based on the previous census because the latest census report is saying that my 'Islamic' centre consists of sixty crore (600 million) souls, and the 'Indian' one consists of thirty-five crore (350 million).

We are not nationalists but super nationalists, and I as

a Muslim say that 'God made man and the Devil made the nation.' Nationalism divides; our religion binds. No religious wars, no crusades, have seen such holocaust and have been so cruel as your last war, and that was a war of your nationalism, and not my *Jehad*.[20]

Thus, there are two sets of issues before us. The first one is personal and eternal in nature, while the second one is temporal and special. The first one is related to the salvation of the populace from the eternal wrath of the Creator, the removal of dirt from spiritual life, achievement of real progress in both the worlds and the attainment of eternal happiness. This is the goal of Islam and its founder. To achieve this goal, the universal law of Islam has always been and should be invoked. Even the slightest laxity would not only harm Muslims, but would also prove harmful for the entire humanity.

The second issue is India and the deliverance of its citizens from the problems faced by them. This issue is temporary and special. This problem will continue to bedevil India till the light of the

---

[20]*Select Writings and Speeches of Maulana Mohamed Ali*, compiled and edited by Afzal Iqbal, M.A.

true religion dispels its darkness. However, as I have said earlier, foreign occupation and the selfish rule of the brute (British) nation has pushed Indians—especially Muslims—to the verge of destruction. As W.S. Blunt said:

I have been studying the mysteries of Indian finance under 'the best masters', Government Secretaries, Commissioners, and the rest, and have come to the conclusion that if we go on 'developing' the country at its present rate, the inhabitants will have, sooner or later, to resort to cannibalism, for there will be nothing but each other left them to eat.[21]

As things stand, there would be no way out for Indians in the future except death and destruction which would not be confined to Indian territories only. The dominance and slavery of India would have far-reaching effect on the nations of the East that would not only endanger the independence of Islamic countries, but would also endanger the welfare of Muslims and their very existence as a respectable *qaum*.

[21] W.S. Blunt, *Ideas about India*, London: Kegan Paul, Trench & Co., 1985, Introduction, p. 14.

Indian soldiers, Indian wealth, Indian arms and Indian knowledge and expertise are being used as means to harm the other *qaum*. Peter Freeman, a member of the House of Commons and President of the Common Wealth of India League, once said: 'At times it has been said that if India gains home rule, a terrible fate would overwhelm the common masses. It however won't be a catastrophe bigger than a hundred years of the British rule that befell on them.'[22]

Sir John Shower wrote in 1833, 'Excessively ruinous and destructive policies of the British rule made India and its inhabitants so poor that one finds difficulty in getting precedence.'

Expressing similar sentiments, Sir William Digby wrote in 1901:

Hard as the saying may sound in the ears of the ordinary Englishman, the plunder is proceeding far more outrageously to-day than at any preceding period. The thin whips of the early days of our rule have become bundles of wire thongs; the exactions of Clive and

[22] Extracted from *Indian News*, London, published in *Madina*, Bijnaur, vol. 19, no. 22, 25 March 1930.

Hastings fall into insignificance by the side of the drain which, in ever-augmenting volume, is over-enriching one country at the cost of the life-blood of another.[23]

Volumes written by none other than the British themselves speak of the hardships and trauma that Indians suffered during the cruel and oppressive British regime. Muslims have been the worst victims of its oppression. Therefore, it is the duty of every Indian citizen to strive to overthrow this oppressive regime. It is necessary to use the lesser evil, which Muslims are ordered and authorized to use by the sharia. To fulfil the obligation of *jihad* and execute it, there is no condition of special arms and special method. All those strategies and all weapons that could destroy the enemy, weaken its hold on power and diminish its pomp and grandeur are permissible. It is this meaning that is conveyed through words like *swatantrata* (freedom) and *swaraj* (self rule).

No other *qaum* and country in history has harmed Islam more than Europe in general, and

[23] William Digby, *Prosperous British India*, New Delhi: Sagar Publication, 1969, p. 27.

Britain in particular. In Asia and Africa alone, over 72,74,360 square miles of land were appropriated from Muslims. If Muslim land annexed to Europe were added to it, the figure would be around 90,00,000 square miles. These were those European countries where Christianity was established after overthrowing Islamic rule. All analyses and intelligence prove that composite nationalism is the most effective weapon of Indians against foreign rule. This would harm the British political lords more than anything else. With the passage of time, this has begun to increasingly offend them and had compelled them to devise a poisonous prescription called *Divide and Rule* to counteract this danger. Since the beginning Indians were lured into consuming this fatal poison in sugarcoated pills and even today, this poison is being injected into the body politic of India. It was this that strengthened the British rule in India and it cannot be said when this hegemony will come to an end.

British thinkers like Sir John Maynard and others were alert to danger that composite nationalism could pose to British hegemony in India.

Professor J.R. Seeley in his book entitled, *The Expansion of England*, expressed the same fear in the following words:

Now if the feeling of a common nationality began to exist there only feebly, if, without inspiring any active desire to drive out the foreigner, it only created a notion that it was shameful to assist him in maintaining his dominion, from that day almost our Empire would cease to exist. As it was acquired without much effort on the part of the English state, it must be retained in the same way. We are not prepared to bury millions upon millions or army upon army in defending our acquisition.[24]

British thinkers have propounded many enchanting theories, produced an abundance of literature, distributed countless handbills and organized numerous lectures to misguide simple and clean-hearted Indians. This was a ruse and a stratagem to cripple Indian minds, especially Muslim minds. Something that was described as

[24] J.R. Seeley, *The Expansion of England*, Chicago and London: The University of Chicago Press, 1884.

beneficial for Europe was projected as poisonous for Muslims.[25] Aversion to composite nationalism was instilled in the hearts and minds of Muslims. They were persistently told that this would destroy the spirit of their religion, culture, religious education, unity, etc. Critical comments are made about the adherents of religion and the sharia. The 'ulama engaged in the service of mankind are labelled 'Possessed Bishops'. Interestingly, persons whose practical life did not manifest any religion and religiosity commented sarcastically on those who served Islam and whose life was a model of religiousness.

The magicians (read politicians) of Britain have cast a powerful spell on the hearts and minds of Indians. The powerful spell has entrapped even an intelligent, brave and politically conscious man of the stature of Sir Syed Ahmad Khan, who had not only proved his courage and love for the nation by writing books such as *Asba'b-i-Baghawat-i-Hind* (The Causes for Indian Revolt), but also had the

[25] For details consult articles and lectures of Mr. Beck and Mr. Morrison, Principals of Aligarh College.

courage to say the following about composite nationalism:

The word *qaum* applies to people living in one country. Remember that *Hindu* and *Muslim* are words of religious significance; otherwise *Hindus*, *Muslims* and *Christians* who live in this country are one *qaum*. When these groups are called one *qaum*, their country of dwelling being one, their national interest should be one as well. Days are gone when inhabitants of the same country will be regarded two distinct *aqwam* (nations) on the basis of religion.[26]

On another occasion Sir Syed had said, 'Like Aryans who are called *Hindu*, Muslims, too, are called *Hindu*—that means inhabitants of India.'[27]

He remarked on another occasion, 'The word *Hindu* that you have used for yourself (as a religious community) is not right, in my opinion. In my view, *Hindu* is not the name of any religion. Every one living in India can call himself a *Hindu*. However,

---

[26] 'Majmua Lecture Sir Syed Ahmad Khan' (Collection of Sir Syed's Lecture) and 'Raushan Mustaqbil'.

[27] 'Sir Syed ke A'khri Mazamin' (Last Articles of Sir Syed), p. 55.

it is quite strange and sad as well that though we (Muslims) live in India, you (Hindus) do not consider us Hindu.'[28]

Talking on the issue of Hindu–Muslim unity, Sir Syed said:

I have repeatedly said that India is like a beautiful bride and *Hindus* and *Muslims* are her two beautiful eyes. The beauty lies in safety and equality of both of her eyes. If one of them loses uniformity, the beautiful bride would become ugly. And if one is lost, the same beautiful bride would turn blemished, one-eyed.[29]

Later Sir Syed was so mesmerized and influenced by the enchantment of British magicians like Mr Beck, Mr Morrison and Mr Archapold that he not only ceased to draw people's attention to composite nationalism, but also generated hatred in Muslim minds against it and opposed the Indian National Congress and its policies. He was the

---

[28] 'Safar Nama Punjab' (Sir Syed's Travelogue) and 'Raushan Mustaqbil' (The Bright Future), pp. 139, 271 respectively.

[29] 'Sir Syed ke A'khri Mazamin' (Last Articles of Sir Syed), p. 55.

front-runner among those who provided support to the British government and also considered it the nectar of immortality for Indian Muslims.

It was this sea change in Sir Syed's perception of composite nationalism that Allama Shibli Nomani, his associate for more than fifteen years, was forced to write about in the *Muslim Gazette*, Lucknow:

That strong hand, holding powerful pen, which wrote the book *Asba'b-i-Baghawat-i-Hind* (The Causes for Indian Revolt) at a time when the horrendous heat of Martial Law was raging at its highest peak; that brave man who had shredded into pieces the arguments advanced by Lord Lytton against the Punjab University Bill; that knowledgeable person who pressed for the individual rights in the form of three articles in a language that the literatures produced by the Indian National Congress could not match; that fearless man who walked out of the *Agra Darbar* because the sitting arrangements of Indians and the British were not at par; that justice lover who stood alone in support of Bengalis and bore witness saying that Bengalis are the only *qaum* in this country on whom Indians can justifiably take pride, the surrounding situation and turn of events forced that very man to stop Muslims from taking part in politics. Why did this happen? What were the reasons behind this? To discuss and debate the questions and answers of what brought about this sudden change and differences in him would not only be irrelevant, but harmful as well. This is the time to exercise judgment and emulate those who are busy in freedom struggle.[30]

Thus, the magicians of Britain entrapped a politically conscious and wise man (of Sir Syed's stature) and not only used him to oppose composite nationalism, but also to prevent Muslims from participating in politics and constitutional struggle in order to alienate them from politics forever. It would not be surprising if the same enchanting spell is cast on Mohammad Iqbal too.

The interests of colonialist Britain are known to us; the deceptive moves of their hired men, the wonders and trickery of their propaganda and propaganda machinery are also known to us. Even the mighty kingdoms of Europe have often been entrapped by the strange magic of this imperialist power called Britain. They have openly expressed

[30] 'Raushan Mustaqbil' (The Bright Future), p. 321.

and accepted this fact. Thus, they have not only befooled ordinary people on this planet, but have also cheated great kings and nobles.

In a nutshell, Indians in general and Muslims in particular are in deep trouble these days. To overcome these problems, to prevent such recurrences in the future and to secure a social life that is free from worries is an important issue that is exclusively related to India and its people. This problem is, however, confined to life in this mundane world only. As compared to the life of Hereafter that is eternal, the problem and the life of this world are mere shadows. Composite nationalism is needed only till such time different *aqwam* and different religions exist in a country. When the entire nation becomes Muslim, where is the need for it? I have termed it 'temporal and special' for this reason.

As I have said earlier, it is religiously, sensibly, humanely and politically incumbent upon Indian Muslims to actively participate in both promotion of faith and composite nationalism. Participation in one does not preclude the other. To prevent

Muslims from being a part of composite nation-alism on religious grounds would tantamount to non-participation of Muslims in the struggle for overthrowing British rule. At a time when Muslims are in a minority, this would not only cripple them, but would also lead them to their graves.

All that I have said here also reflects the views of Maulana Mohammad Ali Jauhar and Shaikhul Hind Maulana Mahmood Hasan.

The first issue (religion) is personal and fund-amental and that was the purpose of the Prophet's arrival. Prophet Mohammad invited the Quraish and polytheists of Makkah to come to the fold of Islam. The second issue (composite nationalism) is temporary and individualistic. In spite of the revelation of the *Ayat-e-Jihad* (verses of war) in the holy Koran Prophet Mohammad sought cooperation from the Jewish tribes of Madina. To criticize and comment on such things would prove nothing except ignorance.

The British government is making all-out efforts to prevent Indian Muslims from entering the political field. They do not want Muslims to participate in composite nationalism and become a united force in launching the freedom struggle that may prove a catalyst in overthrowing the British government. Those who are trying to prevent Muslim participation in politics and are trying to paint a hateful picture of composite nationalism, are undoubtedly doing a great service to the British government, which their own army and arsenals have failed to achieve.

That is why I say:

Tarasam Narasi Be Ka'ba Tu Aye E'raabi,
Ke'in Ra'h Ke Tu Mirawi Be Englista'n Ast.

I am afraid, you may not reach Ka'ba O' Bedouins of Arabia!
The path you are treading leads to England.